Teaching Your Kids about

# SEX

## More than a Plumbing Lesson

### Amy Scheuring

⊞ CHRISTIAN PUBLICATIONS, INC.
CAMP HILL, PENNSYLVANIA

## ✛ CHRISTIAN PUBLICATIONS, INC.

3825 Hartzdale Drive, Camp Hill, PA 17011
www.christianpublications.com

*Faithful, biblical publishing since 1883*

*Sex: More than a Plumbing Lesson*
ISBN: 0-87509-980-7
LOC Number: 2003105206
© 2003 by Amy Scheuring
All rights reserved
Printed in the United States of America

03   04   05   06   07      5   4   3   2   1

---

# Dedication

To my Mom and Dad,
who share love for a lifetime.

---

# Contents

# Acknowledgments

Thank you, Tom, Steven and Kathryn. I love you. Thank you to all of the Reality Parenting families who allowed us to learn from their struggles and their victories. Thanks to the hundreds of teenagers and parents who have opened up their hearts to me over the years. And my warm thanks to everyone at Christian Publications, Inc., for believing in this project.

"The test is positive." Imagine the impact of those words on the life of an unmarried teenager. "Not me, not now, not a baby," she sobs in disbelief. Her worst fears are now confirmed and life's possibilities have been limited to four options: abortion, adoption, single parenting or early marriage. Her future plans derailed, she faces a decision that will change the rest of her life. The slogan "a woman's choice" has already sent her boyfriend to the sidelines. While the future of his child is being determined, he'll watch as a helpless spectator. Would-be grandparents wonder where they went wrong and do their best at damage control.

As the director of a busy pregnancy crisis center, I found myself delivering this news to couples on a daily basis. The people I met with were faced with difficult circumstances that had no perfect solutions. My job was to help young women make the best possible decision for themselves and their growing baby and then provide all that they would need to ease the path they chose.

"If only I could talk to kids before they needed a pregnancy test," I'd pray. "If only I could reach them before they began to experiment with sex. If only I could talk to their parents." Within my first year as director of the pregnancy center, I was asked to speak to a large group of teens about the power of abstinence. I wondered how they would react. Was I dreaming, or was it possible for a teen to live a pure life?

## Parenting for Purity

Within the first five minutes of my presentation, I had my answer. Instead of rolling eyes or snickers from the group, I
heard sighs of relief. I even heard someone say, "You mean I
don't *have* to do it?" One girl walked right up to me afterward
and said, "This is the best news I've ever heard."

It was also the best news a lot of teens had *never* heard.
Safe sex, not abstinence, was the message of the late 1980s.
Condoms could be found at every school nurse's office and
AIDS education became mandated by most states. Abstinence speakers were rare in those days. Fifteen years later
that has changed. Teens by the thousands are now hearing
about sexual purity. Through videotapes, national programs, high-profile speakers and school-based abstinence
programs, schools and youth groups are informing and mo-
tivating young people to choose sexual purity.

It is surprising to me, however, that many teens are not
hearing about abstinence from the most effective source:
their parents.

## Awesome Privilege

The presentation I most enjoy leading is called "Created
in Love." It is the talk where fifth grade girls get together
with their moms to find out about growing up, menstrua-
tion, shaving their legs and other girl stuff. It's one of life's
golden moments, when mother and daughter share an inti-
mate secret with laughter and tears. Later, at the cookie table, I often hear the moms' familiar comments: "I wish
someone would have talked to me when I was a kid," or "I
learned about this from the school nurse and a film strip" or
"My mom never told me a thing." They seem to know instinctively that sex education is best taught by parents. I
heartily agree.

You, as parents, are the primary sex educators in your children's lives. No one on this earth can do a better job than you. Even if you never say a word (but especially if you do), you are teaching sexual values and modeling behavior. What an awesome privilege; what an incredible responsibility. It makes me wonder why parents would give the job to anyone else.

As our children approach adolescence, the questions they raise about sex and sexual development become more and more complex. These questions quickly take the discussion beyond the mere "plumbing" lesson of body parts, functions and development to issues and situations that leave you groping for the right thing to say. How will you answer them? What will you say and when?

In our sex-saturated culture, the stakes are higher than they used to be. Teen pregnancy, abortion and sexually transmitted diseases are now an epidemic. Parents long for wisdom about where to set the boundaries and need the confidence to raise a higher standard in a world where "everyone's doing it." But who will equip you for this terrific challenge? Your parents? Your peers? Dr. Laura?

## Reality Parenting

Parents do not instinctively know what warning signs to look for when things aren't going well, nor do they know the signs of a healthy and flourishing teenager.

So, naturally, we look to the families with experience and success for clues and insight. Proverbs 24:6 tells us, "By wise counsel you can wage your war, and in an abundance of counselors there is victory and safety" (AMP). Throughout this book you'll meet parents who have wrestled with the issues of purity and sexual abstinence and survived.

There is nothing particularly remarkable about these parents—they are just ordinary people fighting a war for their families in the daily dilemmas and decisions involved in raising kids. You will find that each of the parents who share their stories has looked to an authority higher than himself or herself for guidance and wisdom. These "counselors" have been there, they've done their best and they are still pretty much sane.

It is my hope that this book and the stories and information in it will help you separate the truth from fiction, and that you'll be encouraged and equipped for the vitally important work of parenting your children.

There are dozens of great books on the subject of sexuality and parenting, many of which I have cited in the chapters ahead. However, in my search to find the best answers to kids' toughest questions about sex, there is one source in which I consistently find direction, comfort and wisdom: the Bible. When we read and study the Bible, we read God's own words written for us. The Bible is timeless, authoritative and true.

You'll find that I refer to the Bible throughout this book, and so do the many Reality Parenting families you'll meet. If using the Bible is new to you, take a moment to get familiar with it and you will soon learn that you can't live without it.

## Get Familiar with the Book

The Bible is one large book which is made up of sixty-six smaller books. You can find a list of these books at the front of the Bible. They are divided into the Old Testament, or Old Covenant (these are books written before Jesus was born), and New Testament (books written about Jesus' life and the development of the early Christian Church). Some of these books give accounts of historical events, some are poetic and lyrical, some give eyewitness reports of events as they happened and some are letters that encourage and teach.

*Learn how to look up passages.* Each book of the Bible is divided into chapters, and each chapter is divided into verses. When a refer-

## Using the Bible

ence from the Bible is made, it is written as book, chapter and verse. For instance, to look up John 3:16, you would find the book of John using the table of contents, then find the third chapter and then the sixteenth verse.

*Find a Bible that you can read.* There are many great translations of the Bible today. Find an authoritative version of the Bible to have as your own. You may want to look for one that has application notes or one that includes study aids like a concordance or an index to help you find verses.

*Build a habit.* Develop a routine of reading the Bible on a daily basis. Start with a short book like John or Philippians and begin by reading a small section every day. Pray that God will help you understand what He wants to say to you in that passage. You may want to use a highlighter or pen to mark verses that stand out or relate to your life. I like to put a tiny date in the margin so I can look back and see what was meaningful at different times in my life.

Your children are watching. When they see you turning to God's Word for guidance, they will learn to go there too.

**one**

As for you, you were dead in your transgressions and sins, in which you used to live when you followed the ways of this world . . . but because of his great love for us, God, who is rich in mercy, made us alive with Christ even when we were dead in transgressions. (Ephesians 2:1-2, 4-5)

## What Your Parents Told You About Sex

I f you want to get a lively discussion going among adults, ask them this question: "What did your parents teach you about sex?" Many people will begin by answering, "My parents told me nothing . . . nothing at all." But after thinking for a moment or two, they will remember small ways that their mom or dad tried to communicate the basic facts.

Women generally remember a big blue box, a story about an egg and bleeding once a month. Men's experiences range from the vague to the desperate. Some recall an obscure baseball analogy (first base, second, third and then around to "score" at home), some remember confusing references to birds and bees and some were even subjected to such extreme tactics as visits to hookers. One young dad revealed that his father used two

## A Look Back

"frisky" farm animals as a visual aid, awkwardly stating, "That's how people do it, son." That somewhat confusing comparison was the extent of the young man's instructions on the facts of life.

The reality is that your parents were probably no more equipped to discuss sex than you are. That may be the root of why *you* feel less than confident about what to say to *your* kids.

Most of our parents raised families in the face of the 1960s' sexual revolution. They saw the birth of *Playboy*, the rise of feminism, the marketing of the birth control pill and the legalization of abortion through *Roe vs. Wade*. Mainstream America was not prepared for these changes. At that time, *Starsky and Hutch* was the worst thing on TV and drive-in movies were places you took your kids. Parents who were raising children in the innocent world of Mayberry were forced to face the gritty reality of child pornography, date rape, abortion, teen suicide and AIDS. Generally speaking, parents said less and less about sex, hoping that if they didn't talk too much about it, it wouldn't happen.

Ironically, in the early 1960s schools stepped in to fill the silence. The premise for sex education at school, in direct contrast to the approach taken by many parents, seemed to be: "If we talk about sex a lot, it won't happen." Many of us now in our thirties and forties were the first guinea pigs for the well-funded state and federal sex-ed programs.

Thinking back on those early days of sex education, I clearly remember a ninth-grade civics assignment. It was matching, and I loved matching—just draw a line from the word in column A to connect it to a corresponding word in column B. But this exercise was not about state capitals or the three branches of government. Instead, we were to match the proper name of a sexual body part to its corresponding street slang. Everyone else in the class eagerly launched into the unexpected break from boring old civics class, but I was overwhelmed by embarrassment. I didn't know most of the terms in column A and was totally mystified by what appeared in column B. After twenty minutes or so, the teacher collected the papers. As he came to my row, I tucked the blank worksheet into my notebook. *I'll turn it in tomorrow,* I thought. *He'll never notice.* That evening I showed my mother the strange assignment and asked if she could help me out. I never saw the worksheet again. Two weeks later, my dad was running for a spot on the school board, and next thing I knew, the civics teacher wouldn't even speak to me. I "sat out" the rest of "Human Growth and Development" in the resource room.

Twenty-three-year-old author Wendy Shalit had a similar experience in the fourth grade.

> I sat out sex education in the library. I always felt bad for the girls who didn't have this escape because after each sex ed session, the boys would pick on them, in a strange, new kind of teasing. . . . For some reason, no one connects this kind of harassment and early sex education. But to me the connection was obvious from the start, because the boys never teased me— they assumed I didn't know what they were referring to. Whenever they would start to tease me, they always stopped when I gave them a confused look and said, "I have no idea what you guys are talking about. *I* was in the library." Even though I usually did know what they were talking about, the line still worked, and they would be almost apologetic: "Oh, right— you're the weirdo who always goes to the library."

And they would pass me by and begin to torture the next girl, who they knew had been in class with them and could appreciate all the new put- downs they had learned. All across North America, sex educators are doling out such ammunition under the banner of enlightenment.[1]

Under the "banner of enlightenment," schools taught about monthly cycles, ejaculation, correct names for sexual "plumbing" and how to use birth control. And, because the job was in the capable hands of the "sexperts," parents said next to nothing. Perhaps you'd like to do things differently.

# Zoom in

- Think back to when you were a teenager. How did you find out about sex? Check all that apply:

| | |
|---|---|
| _____ my mom | _____ my dad |
| _____ my boyfriend/ girlfriend | _____ my friends |
| _____ pornography | _____ books/movies |
| _____ school sex ed | _____ church/religious instruction |

- From the list above, which two sources most shaped your *values* about sex?

- How did your parents handle the job of teaching you about sex? Rate them from one to ten.

- What obstacles to educating you about sex do you think your parents faced as you grew up?

- What were the pros and cons of the sex education you received in school?

In September of 1997, *The Journal of the American Medical Association* published the results of a long-term study on teens and behavior. *The National Longitudinal Study on Adolescent Health (Ad Health)* revealed five keys to reducing teen sexual behavior and pregnancy. School sex education was not among them. The factors that contribute most to the delay of sexual activity have to do with good parenting. Family connectedness, parental disapproval of their child being sexually active and parental disapproval of their adolescent using birth control were the top three deterrents to teenage sexual activity. (Notice that parental disapproval of sexual activity and disapproval of their kids using birth control are two separate messages that need to be conveyed in a clear way.) The other two key factors in delaying sex were church involvement and using an abstinence pledge.[2]

The conclusion of the study was clear: A child who feels connected to his or her home and who understands the rules of the house is less likely to experiment with sex or look for love outside of the home. That's because sex education is *values* education. You, as parents, are the only people who hold all of the keys identified in the study. You are the most effective influence in your child's sexual development. And you *are* up to the challenge.

## Notes:

1. Wendy Shalit, *A Return to Modesty: Discovering the Lost Virtue* (New York: The Free Press, 1999), pp. 17-8.
2. Michael D. Resnick, et al. "Protecting Adolescents from Harm: Findings from the National Longitudinal Study on Adolescent Health," *The Journal of the American Medical Association*, Vol. 278 (10), September 10, 1997, pp. 823-32.

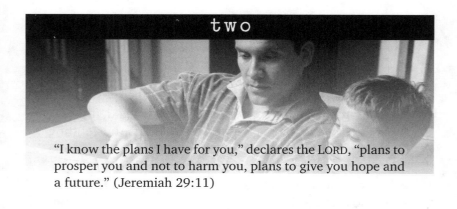

## two

"I know the plans I have for you," declares the LORD, "plans to prosper you and not to harm you, plans to give you hope and a future." (Jeremiah 29:11)

Everyone's doing it, right? Most sex-ed curricula assume that to be fact. They assert that all kids are going to have sex and then conclude that we might as well give kids all of the information on birth control that we can so they can do it safely without fear of pregnancy or AIDS. This is an easy assumption to make when you've been raised on a steady diet of evolution and moral relativism that basically says, "You have evolved from lower animals; therefore you are an animal; therefore you can do nothing other than behave like an animal." Under this system, there are no absolutes, no right and wrong, so sex before marriage is something you do when you feel like you are ready. Children are put in the same category as bunnies: little breeders with no higher purpose, no conscience, no constraint.

These lessons lead today's parents to what seems like a logical conclusion: that they might as well prepare their kids to do it right, because they know that kids are going to do it anyway. Perhaps you recall a national news story about a woman who was arrested for equipping her thirteen-year-old son with condoms. There was a

# Sex in the Real World

huge public debate over the story. Some felt she was being
a responsible parent, protecting her boy from the ravages of
disease and taking responsibility to avoid the possible im-
pregnation of a young girl. Others were outraged, insisting
that to provide condoms was to condone sex, thus putting
her child in harm's way. Sex education faces the same
mixed reviews. One side says, "Isn't it responsible to give
kids access to information and birth control?" The other
says, "Doesn't this information encourage kids to make un-
wise choices?"

Most schools take the middle ground by offering "comprehensive" sex education, which includes abstinence. But,
if our schools are teaching abstinence, why do we continue
to see a rise in teen pregnancy and STDs? I visited a local
ninth-grade classroom to hear a speaker present the "abstinence" message. She started out by emphatically stating
that abstinence is the only 100% effective way to avoid
pregnancy and disease. But, she continued, if you are going
to have sex, you'll need to consider the thirteen methods of
birth control and protection so you can be safe and responsible. Forty seconds on abstinence and forty minutes on the
"but." (When discussing this topic, I have often referred to
her as the lady with the big "but.")

Teens know that we spend time on what we value. The
"take away" from that lesson was that it's much more likely
that teens will have sex than that they won't, so they should
be sure to do it correctly.

After almost thirty years and $30 million in state and
federal funds, we have learned that this kind of mixed
message doesn't work.

During the last fifteen years of teaching abstinence, I
have found that teens do as they are told. Throughout the

1980s and '90s, teens were told to have safe sex. They learned their lessons well. Outercourse, mutual masturbation and grind dancing (once reserved for strip clubs and adult bookstores) became part of the fabric of teen culture. Kids were being bombarded from all sides with the idea that as long as it wasn't intercourse it was OK. Even the government was sending that message. Look at the Clinton administration, for example—in its final years children learned that oral sex is not really sex. Within two years of the highly-publicized Clinton sex scandal, the number of students I met who had experimented with oral sex at clubs, parties and school (yes, school) skyrocketed.

It is certain that our kids are learning about sex from the culture around them. Look at these facts on teen sexual behavior in the 1990s (remember this is all after almost thirty years of comprehensive sex education):

- Ten percent of teenage girls become pregnant by age eighteen, and teen pregnancy is the number one reason teenage girls go to the hospital.[1]

- Seventy percent of non-marital teen pregnancies are fathered by men older than twenty.[2]

- 30,000 Americans acquire a sexually transmitted disease (STD) every day, making STDs the most widely reported infections in the U.S.[3]

- Teens and young adults ages fifteen to twenty-four are at greatest risk for acquiring an STD.[4]

Teen pregnancy, disease, heartbreak, poor relationships, homosexuality, divorce, depression: These are the lifetime consequences of the safe sex approach. The children have done only as they were told.

So if children are going to do as we say, why don't we tell them how to remain sexually pure? Thankfully, many people have stepped up to do just that. In fact, when the doors finally began to open for school curricula that taught abstinence, the numbers started to turn around. Look what happened when we began to tell kids the truth about sex and equip them to choose sexual purity:

- More than ninety-three percent of teens think it is important for teens to be given a strong message from society that they should abstain from sex until they are at least out of high school.[5]

- Sixty-three percent of ninth- through twelfth-graders have never had sex or are currently abstinent, and fifty percent of high school students (ninth through twelfth grade) report that they have never had sex.[6]

- Seventy-five percent of seventh- through twelfth-graders report that they have never had sex.[7]

- Students who signed pledge cards after abstinence presentations were shown to postpone sexual activity for an average of eighteen months longer than students who did not.[8]

A poll conducted by *Time* and Nickelodeon in 2001 found that seventy-six percent of young teenagers (ages twelve to fourteen) say it's "somewhat or very important" to delay the initiation of sexual intercourse until marriage. The attitudes of older teens are shifting as well. An annual survey of college freshman at the University of California at Los Angeles this past year showed sixty percent—the highest in the history of the survey—said they do not believe it's OK for two people to have sex even if they "really like each other."[9]

It seems that the abstinence message is taking hold in the hearts of teens. But what about their parents? The same *Time*/Nickelodeon poll asked the minority of twelve- to fourteen-year-olds who do believe premarital sex can be OK how old somebody should be before first participating in intercourse. They set the age at a conservative twenty-three years of age. When the pollsters asked the kids' parents the same question, the parents said age eighteen.

Why do so many teens today have more conservative views toward sex than their parents? Dr. Joe McIlhaney, from the Medical Institute for Sexual Health, offers his perspective:

> Maybe it's because too many parents don't fully appreciate how much more dangerous early sexual activity is today than when they came of age twenty or thirty years ago. There are twenty-five STDs today, as opposed to two in 1960. In the 1970s, one adolescent in forty-seven contracted a STD. Today, that figure is one in four. And the STDs are much more dangerous. At least one can kill. Others have been linked to cancer.[10]

Many adults are stuck in the '80s when it comes to questions about sex and teens. Just like the lady with the big "but," they have accepted the "safe sex" messages intended to reduce AIDS transmission as the only way to reduce risk to teens. These parents say:

- "I'm a good parent. My kid isn't in any trouble sexually. He's a good kid; I trust him. Why would I punish him with rules and limits?"

- "I want my daughter to be popular, to have friends. Her friends are good kids from good families."

- "He knows right from wrong."

- "We have a good relationship going. I don't want to rock the boat by arguing about his personal life."
- "Teens are young adults—they need their independence."
- "It's not my place to pry. My daughter will lose respect for me if I invade her privacy."
- "Too many rules make kids rebel."

Have you heard these words? Maybe you've even said these very things. Many parents want to believe that poor sexual choices are only made by *someone else's* teenager. Promiscuity, oral sex, sexually transmitted diseases, pregnancy—these are problems in other families, not yours, right? Now listen to the words of teens raised in families just like yours, whose parents chanted, "It won't happen to my kid" as if those magic words would make the future secure.

- Darcy, thirteen years old, from Los Angeles: "Oral sex has just gotten too boring out here. Most of the popular kids have done sex, or a little of it anyway."
- Marcia, twelve, from Santa Monica: "The eighth graders who've done it say it's disgusting. They spit it out. But they say you just close your eyes, it's over, like, in two minutes, and then people are kind of respected—you're suddenly more experienced and asked for advice. It's kind of a rite."
- James, fifteen, from suburban New York: "Girls want to prove to themselves that they're hot stuff, that they can get who they want. Girls can be ho's [slang for whores] or prudes within limits. And it's OK for a girl not to hook up [read: have sex] if they go to a party, but for guys it's a test of masculinity."[11]

# Counter-**Culture** Parenting

Not long ago, I was asked to address a group of concerned parents at a local school district. I was supporting a team of health teachers who had strongly promoted sexual purity in the ninth-grade health classes. The audience I spoke to represented various views on parenting and sex education. Some parents were extremely permissive about alcohol, sex and curfews. Others were concerned about morals being taught in the schools. Just as the crowd was beginning to get ugly, a community rabbi stood and spoke. He told of a recent *bar mitzvah* where he walked in on several twelve- and thirteen-year-olds who were drunk and engaging in group oral sex. When the parents at this meeting heard that, they were visibly shocked. "When we were all young," he said, "and our parents would take us to a party or to the mall, their warning was clear: 'Be good. Remember who you are!' But today's kids are given a different charge. We say, 'Have fun!' It seems we want our kids to have fun much more than we want them to be good."

Do you want your child to be good? We must accept that being a "good" (in this case, sexually pure) kid may mean a sacrifice of popularity, dates and what passes for fun in the teen culture. Your child may be teased or excluded from "cool" parties. Other parents may criticize you as overly protective, unrealistic and out of touch. One mother put it this way: "I see a lot of parents who want to be cool parents with cool kids. Their biggest concern is popularity, so they don't interfere or say no. I feel like my job is to set up a safety net under my kids so that if they do fall, it won't be life-threatening. Sometimes that 'net' means my kid is not going to end up in the cool crowd. If we ignore what is going on, we may become popular with our kids, but we won't be good parents."

Your child's friends may not value pure behavior. Look at the current perceptions of the sexually active teen: You're fired up, independent, exploring different men or women, not hung up about sex, comfortable with your body, playing the field, capable of handling adult relationships and on and on and on. How does our culture "reward" those who choose sexual purity? They are seen as sexually repressed, bound up, shy or confused, judgmental and hopelessly caught in an archaic Victorian mind-set. They may even be perceived as gay or abused, as having a poor body image or as being overly religious and totally unrealistic. The pressure to fit in to the first list is obvious. If our kids notice that we care more about their popularity than their character, the temptation will be overwhelming.

The Christian faith is revolutionary; it goes against the culture. We, as Christians, are going to stand out in the crowd, and so will our kids. First Peter 2:9 calls Christians a "peculiar people" (KJV). Commitment to high sexual standards is going to cost. But, keep in mind that what your kids sacrifice in terms of party invitations or dates can't be compared to the strength, self-respect and joy they'll one day reap. Good parenting means hours of listening, asking open-ended questions, setting reasonable limits and actively leading your kids to a pure lifestyle. It is more important to be caring than to be cool.

## Open up your questions.

Talking to your kids about sex and dating is ninety percent listening and ten percent talking. How do you get your child to open up about his or her personal life? Try asking good questions.

## Poor Questions

A poor question will be answered in one word, usually "yes" or "no." It gives no room for discussion. A poor question may also force your child into a corner where lying may seem easier than confrontation. Examples of poor questions are:

- Are you two sleeping together?
- You're not having oral sex, are you?
- Would you ever do that?
- You'll never get a girl pregnant, will you?
- Are you really thinking about going out with *him*?

Statements meant to scare teens into purity are even less effective. They create tension and guilt and often close off communication:

- If I ever catch you doing that, you can forget about coming home.
- I hope you aren't as stupid as that kid.
- If I find out you're sleeping with him, I'll send you to an all-girls' school.
- If you have sex, I'll feel like I really screwed up as a parent.

## Open Questions

A good question opens up a topic and allows your child to express his or her feelings. The question provides you with information, not ammunition. Remember, when asking questions about "delicate" subjects, your tone of voice is just as important as the words themselves. Even an open-ended question can bring a halt to a conversation if it sounds like you are condemning the answer before you even hear it. Keep in mind that this discussion is not a debate—it's a chance to see inside your child's heart without attacking him with judgments or lectures. Ease into the topic by asking some questions about related topics or about other kids' opinions on the subject you would like to discuss. Then move to a more personal level. Some good questions might be:

• What does it mean for a couple to be "serious"?
• What is your opinion about birth control for teens?
• How does a person know when he is ready to start dating?
• What do your friends think about oral sex?
• How do you feel about sex before marriage?

If you hear something in your child's response that indicates an idea or assumption that needs to be corrected or changed, let it go for the moment. After your discussion, think and pray about how you will approach the topic. Within one or two days, come back to the question and respectfully give your side. Don't storm in with guns blazing—that will only make your child feel like he's under attack. You may find that by giving your child this space he may have thought the issue through and may even want to amend his answers.

Write down several open-ended questions that would be appropriate to ask your child, then try to find an opportunity to open up a discussion, using your questions as a guide.

## Notes:

1. R.A. Maynard, ed., *Kids Having Kids: A Robin Hood Foundation Special Report on the Costs of Adolescent Childbearing* (New York: Robin Hood Foundation, 1996), p. 1. Also available on-line at: <http://www.urban.org/pubs/khk/summary.html>.
2. K. Ford, W. Sohn, J. Lepkowski, "American Adolescents: Sexual Mixing Patterns, Bridge Partners, and Concurrency," *Sexually Transmitted Disease,* 2002. 29:13-19.
3. American Social Health Association, *STDs in America: How Many Cases and at What Cost?* (Menlo Park, CA: Kaiser Family Foundation, 1998), pub. 1445.

4. Centers for Disease Control and Prevention, "Tracking the Hidden Epidemics," [on-line], July 3, 2001. May 8, 2003. Available from: <http://www.cdc.gov/ nchstp/od/news/RevBrochure1pdftoc.htm#TRENDS%20BY%20DISEASE>.

5. "The Cautious Generation?" Poll released by the National Campaign to Prevent Teen Pregnancy, April 27, 2000.

6. "Youth Risk Behavior Surveillance" [on-line], *Morbidity and Mortality Weekly Report*, CPC, Vol. 49, No. SS-05, June 9, 2000. October 10, 2002. Available from: <http://www.cdc.gov/mmwr/preview/mmwrhtml/ ss4905a1.htm>.

7. "Sex Education in America: A View From Inside the Nation's Classrooms" [on-line], *Kaiser Family Foundation Report*, September 26, 2000. October 10, 2002. Available from: <http://www.kff.org/content/2000/3048/ Agenda5.PDF>.

8. M.D. Resnick, P.S. Bearman, R.W. Blum, et al., "Protecting Adolescents from Harm: Findings from the National Longitudinal Study on Adolescent Health," *Journal of the American Medical Association*, Vol. 278 (10), September 10, 1997, pp. 823-32.

9. "The Cautious Generation?" Poll released by the National Campaign to Prevent Teen Pregnancy, April 27, 2000.

10. Joe S. McIlhaney, Jr., M.D., "Parents and Adolescent Attitudes" [on-line], *Media Advisories*, February 2001. October 9, 2002. Available from: <http://www.medinstitute.org>.

11. Lucinda Franks, "The Sex Lives of Your Children," *Talk,* February 2000, n.p.

## three

For the grace of God that brings salvation has appeared to all men. It teaches us to say "No" to ungodliness and worldly passions, and to live self-controlled, upright and godly lives in this present age. . . . These, then, are the things you should teach. (Titus 2:11-12, 15)

So what do you say to your child about sex, and when do you say it? Don't you sometimes wish that you had a script with appropriate illustrations that you could deliver to your child in one painless dose? Or, better yet, a video that you could slide in and serve with a big bowl of popcorn? Teaching sexual values, however, is not a single event; it is a life-long experience. Many have tried to produce the perfect short-cut—some have even come close—but all will agree that there is no good substitute for an ongoing parenting process that steadily reveals the wonder and mystery of sexual relationships.

What do you *want* your kids to know about sex? What do they *need* to know? The names of body parts, the changes that will occur in adolescence, where babies come from, etc. Well, what's so scary about that? With a little encouragement, almost any adult is equipped to teach the basic facts of life. But we all know that we are communicating more than a "plumbing" lesson when we are talking to our kids about sex. Teaching kids about sex is not the same as

## Seven <u>Great</u> Things

listing the state capitals or memorizing times tables. Sexuality has an implicit moral connection. As parents, therefore, you are uniquely qualified to provide this "values package" that places sex in a context of faith, family and community.

Two-thirds of what teenagers know about sex, they learned on TV.[1] Have they tuned in to some documentary series on the Discovery Channel? Did PBS offer an objective tutorial program on egg and sperm development? *As if.* Our kids are learning sexual *values* on TV, not sexual facts. Therefore, it is up to us to set this right by dispelling the myths and revealing the truth about marriage, family, commitment, respect and love.

The teenage years are an exciting time and should be joyful years of freedom and discovery. It is a time that abounds with endless possibilities for relationship building and growth. So, make sure you tell your kids the good news about their sexuality. The following are seven great things your kids need to know about sex.

## 1. The sex drive is `natural`.

People are prewired to desire relationship, family and community. An increased attraction to and appreciation for the opposite sex is a natural part of adolescence. In Genesis, God was busy creating all of what we know and don't know about our universe. The first day, He said, "Let there be light" (1:3) and there was light. Over the next few days, God created the foundations for everything on earth, and at the end of each day He declared, "It is good!" On the sixth day, after creating all of the animal kingdom, God created Adam and then Eve (1:26). They were fashioned with all of the body parts and hormones men and women are equipped with today. Imbedded in their humanness was an intense desire to love and to be loved intimately with no shame and no fear.

Many people think that God is against sex, and I have come across many young people who actually think that the sinful "eating of the apple" in the garden (3:1-8) was the sex act. Nothing could be further from the truth! After creating man, His masterpiece, God looked at this naked couple and told them to "be fruitful and increase in number" (1:28). It was the first command in the Bible: Go and enjoy sex so that you can have children—and lots of them! At the end of the day, "[He] saw all that he had made, and it was very good" (1:31).

Do you realize that Jesus also had a natural sexual drive? Hebrews 4:14-15 tells us that Jesus was "in *every* way" tempted but without sin. He was fully human and was outfitted with the same natural desires that every young man knows. He can relate to *every* area of temptation because He's already faced it and won. When kids feel overwhelmed by sexual pressure, they can look to the "author and perfecter of our faith" (Hebrews 12:2).

## 2. The sex drive is powerful.

There's no question that we are dealing with a powerful drive, teeming with intense feelings and desires. We may feel like we absolutely have to have it sometimes, but sex is a *drive*, not a *need*. I've never seen an obituary that listed abstinence as the cause of death, have you? The physical urges we feel are very strong, but they are not needs like our need for food, water and shelter.

Keep in mind, however, that even though sex is a drive and not a need, we must be careful of what we feed it. A steady diet of sexual messages and images will fuel a lustful thought life and increase sexual appetite. By feeding an already powerful drive, we can severely limit our ability to discipline our actions. Imagine trying to win a bicycle race after spending a week on the couch eating corn curls and watching TV. You wouldn't have a chance. But if you train and eat properly through the week, winning becomes an attainable goal.

Teens are highly influenced by the media they consume. If they listen to suggestive lyrics, are subjected to sexual themes in other media or are placed in sexually-charged situations, their sexual desires will become heightened. After weeks or months of this kind of input, maintaining sexual purity will be next to impossible even for the strongest of kids. If you want to see them succeed on "race day," you'll have to help them control what they feed their drives.

## 3. The sex drive is controllable.

People are not animals. This may come as a surprise to your children, who have probably been bombarded with lessons on evolution at school, but we are not gorillas in Reeboks. Human beings are made in God's image and have the unique capability to refrain from sex. Many people have questioned my work, suggesting that teens can't help themselves, that they're bound to have sex so we might as well give them birth control. However, a quick look at cultures all over the world down through the ages shows us that sexual control is not only attainable, it has been the expected standard in every healthy civilization.

Remember toilet training? You taught your very young children that they cannot act on every impulse or desire. They learned to control and discipline various urges and to choose appropriate action. We must have confidence that our adolescent children are able to make good choices about sex. This natural, powerful drive is something we as humans *can* master.

Controlling our passions is not the easy choice. Even King David had his faltering moments. Confessing his weak nature to God, he asks, "How can a young man keep his way pure?" (Psalm 119:9). Through God's Spirit, David answers his own question: "By living according to [God's] Word." Throughout Psalm 119, we see the power that the daily reading and understanding of God's Word can bring to a young person struggling with sexual pressures.

The Bible character Job is best remembered for his patience through testing. His upright life before, during and after his trials is inspiring. "I have made a covenant with my eyes," Job states, "not to look lustfully at a girl" (Job 31:1). He could confidently tell his friends and accusers how he had mastered lust in his life: by making a solemn promise to control his eyes.

Sexual temptation *will* come into our children's lives. I try to encourage boys by telling them that it is understandable when they can't avoid the first look. If a beautiful young lady walks by in a revealing outfit, only a blind man would miss it. But, I tell them, they *can* avoid the second look. The second look is the look that engages the imagination: It is where lust is born. Job found that he could control the second look. We can inspire our kids to do the same.

## 4. Sex has a context.

Part of the power of sex is the bond that it creates between a man and a woman. To illustrate this bond to your kids, put a piece of duct tape on the hairy part of your forearm. Explain that the duct tape represents sexual intimacy: It really holds a couple together. Have them look at your arm and the duct tape (what a cute couple!). Don't they look close? But then rip the duct tape off your arm. (Ouch!) Explain that while breaking up is always difficult, it is even more painful after a sexual relationship has developed.

Remind your teens that when they date someone, they have two options. They will either get married or break up. There is no other outcome. Now look at the tape. How can you tell it has been used? Well, OK, it has your hair all over it, but what else? When you try to stick the tape on another arm, you will find the tape isn't as sticky as it was originally. After only one application, it has lost the ability to do what it was created to do. Similarly, with each subsequent sexual relationship, it becomes more and more difficult for a person to bond properly with another.

Just like the duct tape, sex is meant for one application only. In a lifelong marriage, sex is more than a pleasurable moment. It is one part of a joyful journey into acceptance and intimacy.

Cohabitation and divorce are so widely practiced today that many have lost hope in marriage. Teens may not see marriage in their future, but their hearts still long for one true love, a soul mate, someone to love and someone who will love them. Teens may think sex will bring them closer to that goal, but we must assure them that sex without commitment leads to heartbreak, jealousy, insecurity and isolation. If a person has sex outside of marriage, the result will be the opposite of what he set out for, and then he will wonder what went wrong. Marriage is intimacy in the context of long-term commitment—openness, nakedness without shame and without fear of abandonment. Marriage is where sex works best and where, over the years, sex becomes more and more fulfilling.

## 5. Sex has a purpose.

Duct tape bonds things together; that's its purpose. Sex provides a powerful bond as well. Intercourse produces a strong physical and chemical reaction as well as an emotional one. Everything in us screams out, "Bond! Love this person; don't let go of this person." It's no wonder that there is so much emotional damage after a breakup or divorce.

Teens have been lied to: They have been told that sex is just physical—just body parts. But we are not animals responding to an uncontrollable urge. We respond to sexual intimacy with the whole person, not just our physical bodies. The bond that is formed is not easily or lightly broken.

Sex has another vital purpose, of course, and that is procreation—having children. In this culture of "safe" sex, where various forms of birth control are handed out with frightening casualness, I often have to remind students that pregnancy is the natural and expected outcome of sexual intercourse. The many types of birth control have fooled us into thinking that sex and reproduction can be separated into distinct intentions; that we can control if and when pregnancy will occur. The studies show, however, that the promised effectiveness of most birth control methods has been based on studies of adult women. The actual effectiveness for teens is much lower.[2] Teens using any method of birth control are fooled into thinking that they are "safe" from pregnancy and disease. This gives them a false sense of security.

When we minimize or remove the important purpose of reproduction, we lose some of the awe, respect and reverence that must be connected with the sexual act. A new life may be conceived, a whole new person created. Sex must be elevated, cherished and shared only with one who would also share a lifetime of partnering and parenting. Inspiring your child with that awesome reality may be just the motivation he needs in order to stop in a moment of passion.

## 6.  Sexual abstinence *is* possible.

God wouldn't ask us to do something without also giving us the ability to do it. He has asked for the unusual, the difficult, the less traveled road, but He has not asked for the impossible. With every temptation there is a way of escape (see 1 Corinthians 10:13). His plan is for our ultimate happiness, and the journey includes self-sacrifice, patience and discipline. In his letters to a young friend named Timothy, Paul compares the man on the journey to a soldier in an army, an athlete in a competition and a hardworking farmer planting a field (see 2 Timothy 2:3-7). When we have a goal, the sacrifice and training have purpose and are easier to endure.

Virginity until marriage is a reasonable, desirable and attainable goal. For centuries, purity was expected until marriage. Just because our culture has rejected the idea doesn't mean teens are no longer capable of waiting. Don't believe me? Ask the over 1 million students who have signed the True Love Waits commitment. In my hometown, hundreds of teens show up at "Silver Ring Thing" events each month and put on a little silver ring to identify their promise to wait for sex until marriage. In 1997, fifty-one percent of graduating seniors reported that they had never had sex.[3]

All indicators predict that this percentage will rise steadily. When sex is saved and virginity is cherished, a young person possesses a beautiful and valuable gift to be given to his future spouse. Like an athlete winning a gold medal or a farmer enjoying his harvest, your son or daughter will enjoy the lifetime rewards of sexual purity.

## 7. Sexual sin is forgivable.

What happens when kids hear the abstinence message too late? What if their experiences have removed the words *purity* and *virginity* from the menu of their life's choices?

If you want to keep an open line of communication with your children, they must trust that you will forgive them for their mistakes. Teens who have been sexually active often feel like a used piece of duct tape—worthless. They may be living with a trashed reputation or dealing with disease, heartache and maybe even pregnancy or the aftermath of an abortion. Though they wrestle with adult issues, there has never been a time when they have needed you, their parents, more. They need to know that not only will you forgive them, but the Lord will also, so that they can move beyond their mistake.

Remember, forgiveness doesn't mean approval of the action. On the contrary, it acknowledges that wrong has been done and then moves forward to deal with the lingering consequences. A forgiving parent seeks help for the damage in his child's past and becomes more protective and watchful of his child's future.

Does God forgive our past? Yes—absolutely. First John 1:9 says, "If we confess our sins, he is faithful and just and will forgive us our sins and purify us from all unrighteousness." He forgave Abraham in Genesis 15, David in Second

Samuel 12, the woman at the well in John 4 and the woman caught in adultery in John 8. Look up these people in your Bible and read the stories of their sins and of their forgiveness. If God will forgive them, He will certainly forgive you and your children.

- Think back to your teen years. If you had heard about the "seven great things," which one would have had the most impact on your life?

- Which of the "seven great things" do your children need to hear right now?

- Make a plan to teach the "seven great things" to your children.

- Plan an event, such as a special night out, to talk about the seven great things. Don't forget your duct tape!

- In addition to that event, plan ways to continue the conversation over the next months and years.

## Notes:

1. Henry J. Kaiser Family Foundation, "Teens, Sex and T.V." [on-line], May 2000. May 22, 2003. Available from: <http://www.kff.org/content/2002/3229>.

2. E.F. Jones and J.D. Forrest, "Contraceptive Failure in the U.S.: Revised Estimates from the National Survey of Family Growth," *Family Planning Perspectives*, 21:3, May/June 1989, p. 103.

3. "Youth Risk Behavior Surveillance" [on-line], *Morbidity and Mortality Weekly Report*, CPC, Vol. 49, No. SS-05, June 9, 2000. October 10, 2002. Available from: <http://www.cdc.gov/mmwr/preview/mmwrhtml/ss4905a1.htm>.

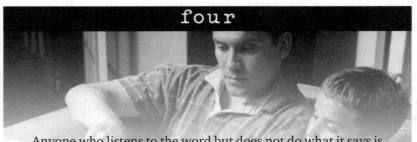

## four

Anyone who listens to the word but does not do what it says is like a man who looks at his face in a mirror and, after looking at himself, goes away and immediately forgets what he looks like. (James 1:23-24)

I magine that you just sat down with your twelve-year-old to discuss the birds and the bees. You've got a plan, a book for handy reference and the nerve. Suddenly your youngster looks up at you and asks, "What did *you* do before you got married? Did *you* wait?"

For some parents, this is the moment they dread. Some have avoided the topic of sex altogether for fear of this question. There is potential for hypocrisy, the revealing of past sins, the loss of credibility in the eyes of their child—all in one painful moment. They feel "busted."

When I first began speaking to teens about sexual purity, I was single and in my late twenties. After my presentation, I would take questions from the audience. Once in a while, a kid would ask me if I'd ever had sex. (Now that I'm over forty, nobody cares what I did before marriage!) I often felt that the answer to that question, no matter what it was, would undermine my entire talk. If I said I was a twenty-seven-year-old virgin, they might discount me as some

## A Look in the Mirror

kind of mutant religious weirdo. At best, they might accept the message only because of the messenger. If I told them that I'd had sex but really regretted the experience and hoped they wouldn't have to repeat my mistakes, they might write off the presentation as hypocritical. I felt I couldn't win.

The fact that I was asked that question showed me that there was an intense desire for a role model, a pioneer. Many of today's abstinence speakers have provided strong role models by using their celebrity status and victorious sexual choices in a most effective package. You may not have celebrity status, but you can still be a role model in your sexual choices—even if you have made mistakes in your past.

There are a wide variety of reasons that parents give for not discussing sexuality with their children. Some may say, "I don't want to be a hypocrite," because they don't feel they can teach sexual purity when at some point in their past (or present) they did not adhere to it themselves. Others may become defensive about their sexual past, saying, "I didn't turn out so bad." Some may even say, "A little experience is good for a kid."

If you have used one of these reasons to avoid discussing sexuality with your child, then you need to take a new look at today's realities. The stakes are simply higher for today's children than they were even fifteen years ago. Our children need to be properly equipped to face the many issues and challenges they come up against, and it is *our* responsibility to do the equipping.

If you did not experience a life of sexual purity before marriage, don't despair. You can raise a standard in your home even if you did not live out that standard in your own past. An admission of sexual activity outside of marriage does not nullify the rules you set today. As for the details, let them remain in the past. And, by all means, do everything you can to live by a higher standard now. Kids spot hypocrisy, but they respect integrity. It is much more important that you provide a good role model today while they are watching.

If and when the question is asked, your discussion should be shifted away from your sexual past and focused on your child's sexual future: What will *he* do? One way to make that shift is to take *corporate* responsibility for the current sexual confusion in today's society by apologizing for the mistakes made by your generation. Even if you were not an active participant in those mistakes, what our culture has allowed and has even celebrated is shameful. Today's teens reap the grim harvest of a counterfeit sexual revolution. We've left them wandering though a battlefield of disease, death and heartbreak. As an adult, you can ask for your child's forgiveness for placing our society's failures in his lap. You could say something like, "Our generation did some foolish things, and unfortunately your generation has inherited the consequences of our mistakes. I apologize for that. But our family is raising a higher standard and we're going to support wise choices."

## Dealing with Your Past

If you are haunted by past failures and drowning in regret, look to the remarkable story told in John 8:1-11 in which Jesus is presented with a woman caught in adultery. Someone had dragged her away from her lover and placed her in front of Jesus as a test of His authority. What would He do with such an obvious law breaker?

The established penalty was death by stoning. The woman cowered in fear, assuming that she would get what she deserved. But then she heard Jesus' remarkable words, "If any one of you is without sin, let him be the first to throw a stone at her" (8:7). The once-eager crowd slowly broke away, leaving the half-naked woman alone with her Judge. His words pierced her heart more deeply than any stone could have pierced her body: "Neither do I condemn you. . . . Go now and leave your life of sin" (8:11).

Does this mean that Jesus gives us a pass when it comes to our sexual sin? Definitely not. It's clear that Jesus cared so much for this woman that He wanted her to leave the lifestyle she was living. His desire was for her to be free, to sin no longer.

Another woman's story is found in Luke 7:36-50. After she finds out Jesus is in the room, this woman falls at His feet, weeping, and pours out an expensive perfume from an alabaster jar. She proceeds to kiss Jesus' feet and wipe them with her hair. This extravagant act is condemned by the onlookers. They make remarks about her character—everyone seems to be aware of "what kind of woman" she is. We don't know what she's done, but her response to Jesus' forgiveness tells us that her sin must have been great. Jesus tells His host, "I tell you, her many sins have been forgiven—for she loved much. But he who has been forgiven little loves little" (7:47).

You too can be free from the guilt of the past. If your failings have been great, then your response to God's forgiveness should be great as well, for He will forgive all of them.

Though you may deal with the ongoing consequences of your sexual choices, a relationship with Christ can give you a second chance—a chance for peace. Leave your past to the One who can give you a future. As Jesus says to the woman, "Your faith has saved you; go in peace" (7:50).

## Zoom in

- Take a long look at your sexual past.
- Be humble and thankful for your victories and forgive yourself for your failures. Read the story in John 8:1-11, then look up and memorize First John 1:9.
- Seek loving help and counsel for serious past events such as incest, abuse or abortion.
- Consider how you will respond to your child's questions and challenges and formulate a response that focuses on your child's future.
- Take a long look at your current sexual behavior. Are you a good role model for your son or daughter? What changes should you make that will positively affect your child's welfare?

## A Standard That is Higher than I

I almost stopped to applaud for a young mom at the grocery store the other day. A defiant toddler was screaming, "Why, why, why?!" after his mother had, for the fourth time, said "no" to the child's plea for a candy bar. In response to her child's wailing, the mother confidently answered the red-faced little fellow, "Because I'm the mom, that's why." End of discussion. It's great to be the authority, isn't it? That mom knew the importance of a final voice, a higher law and the value of respect.

A family must cultivate a healthy respect for authority in the many forms it will take through life. As parents, we must teach our children how to respond to teachers, policemen, pastors, governmental laws and all other authorities that command respect and compliance along life's road. But our long-term job is to raise our kids to one day be independent of our parental authority and to become parents themselves. This journey to adulthood comes in phases, so we should expect some testing of our authority along the way. It may be easy to say "no" to a three-year-old who wants to cross a street or a seven-year-old who wants to drive the family car, but when a teenager asks, "Why, why, why?" about rules concerning dating and sex, our confidence may wane. Discussions may turn to masturbation, homosexuality and setting limits for physical affection. You may think to yourself, "Who am I to say that this or that is right or wrong?" This is the point when a parent needs to seek a higher moral authority.

When David was the king of Israel, he was the highest authority in the land. However, he humbly appealed to the "rock that is higher than I" (Psalm 61:2) for wisdom, direction and protection. We find David, throughout his reign as king, repeatedly seeking the King of kings for answers, for provision and for forgiveness. When your authority is questioned or your past mistakes undermine your confidence, look to the Rock that is higher than you are. Just as a compass needs a steady, solid surface to accurately point north, we need to look to God as our steady place—our Rock. Those around us may base their standards on what feels right at the time, but it shifts with the trends and feelings of the day. We, on the other hand, have a steady place—our Rock—on which we can plant our feet and consistently and accurately point the way.

To give kids a glimpse of that authority, I encourage parents to make a promise to practice chastity. (Don't worry—I'm not in some new cult that enforces unrealistic restrictions on its members.) By chastity I mean sexual purity. By being chaste, we demonstrate to our children that we too comply with God's authority over our sexual choices. Chastity exhibits obedience to the God who made us and loves us. When you are married, chastity means remaining faithful to your spouse with no sex outside the marriage. When you are unmarried, chastity means abstinence until marriage. Chastity is a lifelong value that you can practice and preach. Even if you are a single parent, you can help your kids to understand the sanctity and value of a good marriage by honoring God's plan for abstinence outside of marriage.

When the Apostle Paul wrote to the new Christians in Thessalonica, he reminded them of how they ought to "live in order to please God. . . . It is God's will that you should be sanctified: that you should avoid sexual immorality; that each of you should learn to control his own body in a way that is holy and honorable, not in passionate lust like the heathen, who do not know God" (1 Thessalonians 4:1, 3-5). This may be a difficult step to make—chastity is a challenge at any age. But practice makes perfect, and the earlier we begin to "practice" purity, the better. Many times after I have spoken to teens and their parents, it is a mom or a dad who will approach me and confess that the talk was just what *they* needed to hear. Some adults struggle with purity issues just as much as their teens do. One mom told me that after her divorce she found herself in a string of sexual relationships. She was shocked when she overheard her daughter saying to a friend, "My mom sleeps around, so why shouldn't I?"

Values are not only *taught* in the home, they are *caught*. Are you having sex outside your marriage? Then that has to stop. Do you use pornography? Then get some help to break the habit. Do you promote purity in your home by monitoring TV, Internet and media influences? Do you honor marriage and raise a standard for sexual purity until marriage? If you don't, who will?

## Linda and Ron

Linda and Ron Wells have had a difficult marriage. While they were dating, Linda became pregnant and had an abortion. When she became pregnant a second time, she and Ron decided to marry. Against all odds, they were together for over eighteen years and raised four children. Now separated from Ron, Linda looks back on how her past continues to influence her parenting decisions. We will also hear from her daughter, Keisha, as she reflects on the lessons she learned from her imperfect parents.

**Linda:** I remember sitting down to have a talk with Keisha. She was probably only twelve years old, but I had to get some things out in the open. I was afraid of what she would think of me and Ron. I had already had discussions with Keisha about reproduction and relationships, but this talk was going to be more difficult because I was going to open up about my own past.

### Why that moment? Was Keisha beginning to ask questions?

**Linda:** I had two reasons to bring it all up. Keisha was old enough to do the math. Ron and I had our twelfth anniversary coming up soon after Keisha's twelfth birthday. She began to ask some questions about pregnancy, and I knew that she was figuring out the time line. I had also begun to volunteer at a local pregnancy center with women who had been through an abortion. I was doing a little public speaking on the topic of Post-Abortion Stress. I didn't want my children to hear rumors about Ron and me. I wanted to tell my story at home first.

# The Talk

### *Keisha, your mom revealed some pretty deep, difficult things about her past. How did you respond?*

**Keisha:** Finding out that your parents made some mistakes changes you a little. But I don't remember being disappointed in them. By that time, I knew that my parents loved me very much. I never felt like a "mistake" or that I was unwanted. My parents were very involved at church, and I knew that whatever they had done was forgiven. It was in the past.

### *Did you ever feel that they were hypocritical?*

**Keisha:** No, never. They raised very high standards for us. I was not encouraged to date at all. My dad was very strict about that: No dating until age sixteen. He set the rules at home and we accepted that. It made me feel sort of protected. As I grow up, I see why they were strict with us—they wanted us to avoid all the mistakes they had made.

### *Was it hard to stick to the rules?*

**Keisha:** At times it was tough to trust that they were right. Some rules seemed pointless. I can remember having a crush on this guy in junior high. I wanted to wear something he would notice. My dad saw the outfit I was wearing and told me to go back to my room and put some clothes on. I thought I looked cute. My mom took me aside and told me that my self worth would never come from a boyfriend. She said I was "above all that," that I was worth so much more than a look from a boy. I never forgot that.

### *And now?*

**Keisha:** Now that I'm in college, I see the wisdom in my parents' rules about postponing dating. So many girls depend on their boyfriends to make them feel like something. They are so insecure if they don't have a guy in their life. I have lots of friends; we hang out, get silly and have fun without the pressure of sex.

## Do guys ask you out?

**Keisha:** All the time. They want to hook up and I tell them I'm above all that! I'm looking for a guy with strong values, commitment to his family and a strong focus on service to God. It's easy now to say "no" to guys who just want the physical stuff. I also wear a promise ring that symbolizes my commitment to sexual purity.

## Where did you get the ring?

**Keisha:** From my parents, of course. It constantly reminds me of their love for me and the commitment I've made to wait until I'm married.

## Linda, what do you think helped Keisha get to this point?

**Linda:** We were loving but strict parents. I think kids respond to rules. The other key is good friends. Keisha has a core group of friends that support each other. They are her lifeline. And these kids are respected. They are the kids that others turn to for advice or opinions.

## It sounds like you haven't let your past failures interfere with your vision.

**Linda:** We've made mistakes and we continue to pay for some of those mistakes in our marriage. At this point, Ron and I have had to put our differences aside for the sake of our kids. We worked hard to keep our relationship together. Even now that we are separated, we have to make careful choices because we know the kids are watching. We're not perfect, but we are forgiven.

# five

All Scripture is God-breathed and is useful for teaching, rebuking, correcting and training in righteousness, so that the man of God may be thoroughly equipped for every good work. (2 Timothy 3:16-17)

**M**ost researchers, pollsters and sex educators (even those with the best intentions for your kids) have based their vision for sexual education on current assumptions about sexuality. But cultural trends, shifting values and a media-driven concept of "normal" sexual behavior create a poor foundation to build a framework for lifetime sexual values. Your picture of sex must be brought into full light, based on something timeless, constant and unchanging. But where do you go with your questions about love, relationships, dating and sex?

The people of the Bible had questions about these issues too. Paul responds to a letter from the people living in Corinth to shed light on their questions. And what are the Corinthians asking about? Sex, of course. At that time, Corinth was sin city. (As a matter of fact, people in nearby cities referred to promiscuous men and women as "Corinthians" just as we might use the degrading word *slut*.) So how does the Apostle Paul answer their questions? Look at First Corinthians 7:1-2 in The Message:

## Improve Your Lighting

Now, getting down to the questions you asked in your letter to me. First, is it a good thing to have sexual relations? Certainly—but only within a certain context. It's good for a man to have a wife, and for a woman to have a husband. Sexual drives are strong, but marriage is strong enough to contain them and provide for a balanced and fulfilling sexual life in a world of sexual disorder.

A world filled with sexual disorder—sounds like our world, doesn't it? To answer the questions of the past as well as address the struggles of today, God revealed His timeless truths in His Word. The Bible is abiding and authoritative, spanning generations yet current for today and you'll find that it contains far more about sex than you thought.

A boy in my seventh-grade Sunday school group had decided to start reading the Bible cover-to-cover. After he finished Genesis, I asked him how it was going. His face flushed red, then purple, as he confessed, "I never knew there was so much sex in the Bible!" Who knew? The Bible is like an owner's manual for the human race. Struggles arise, fashions fade, trends come and go, but God never changes.

In our house, we have a well-worn dictionary. During their preschool years, if my kids asked me what a word meant, I would pull the dictionary off the shelf and read them the definition. Through the years, they've come to rely on that same dictionary themselves. After all, why should they take my word for it when there's an authoritative resource so handy? Similarly, if your kids see you searching through the Bible for answers, they will learn to go there too. The Word of God gives a standard that is *above us* and places God as the authority on how to live our lives. If they go to the light of the Word consistently, they will find

- that God created sex and called it "very good" (Genesis 1-2);
- that God gave the people He loved specific laws to provide them with the most fulfilling sexual experience possible (Leviticus 18);
- that they can resist temptation like Joseph did in Potiphar's house (Genesis 39);
- that even people who love God, like King David, may experience failure and defeat (2 Samuel 11-12);
- that God forgives sexual sin when we ask (Psalm 51);
- that the passion and excitement in the Song of Solomon belong in a marriage (Song of Solomon 1-8);
- that children are a blessing from God (Psalm 127:3-5);
- that Jesus had a sex drive but did not act on it (Hebrews 4:14-15);
- that Jesus loved sinners and spent time ministering to prostitutes (Matthew 9:10-12);
- that Paul could remain single and abstinent (1 Corinthians 7:7-8);
- that we can do all things through Christ who strengthens us (Philippians 4:13).

Your reliance on God's standards and biblical authority make it possible for you to confidently set limits for your children's sexual behavior. We are to live by God's standards, not by ones tossed by the winds of our culture.

It may feel unnatural at first to go to the Bible for advice on sex; after all, when it comes to sex, Christianity is often misrepresented. It has been viewed as a fun-killing, Victorian, out-of-touch religion that oppresses women and represses sexual expression. But nothing could be further from the truth! Christianity elevates women to equal ground with men, a notion which is unheard of in any other religion of middle-eastern origin. Young Mary, the mother of Jesus, was the first to know of Jesus' coming (Luke 1:26-38). The woman at the well in John 4 was one of the first people to hear that Jesus was indeed the Messiah (4:1-26). Women were the first to hear the news that He had risen from the dead (Luke 23:55-24:10). Jesus touched women who were considered unclean (Mark 5:25-34). He healed them, forgave them and honored them (Luke 7:36-50). He condemned the abuse of women (Mark 12:38-40) and demonstrated care for women of all ages.

He elevated and affirmed marriage, denounced frivolous divorce (Mark 10:2-9) and performed His first recorded miracle at a wedding reception (John 2:1-11). The Bible clearly reveals that marriage is the context for sex (Hebrews 13:4) and that sex is for pleasure as well as procreation (Song of Solomon 7:6-13). God calls us His Bride and describes Himself as our Bridegroom (Ephesians 5:25-33).

It's time to take a fresh look at what the Christian faith really says about sex. When I speak to teen audiences in a religious setting, I give them the following "Top Twelve Scriptures." I feel it is the best tool I can put in their hands.

# Top Twelve Scriptures to Keep You Pure

1. Genesis 1:26-31—God invented sex and considered it "very good"! Genesis 2:20-24 tells us that sex has a context; it is marriage.
2. Exodus 20:14—In the Ten Commandments, the Lord clearly says, "Don't have sex with someone you are not married to." This command is expanded in Leviticus 18.
3. Psalm 101:1-3—"I will set before my eyes no vile thing" (101:3). What are your eyes looking at? Guard your eyes. Guard your heart.
4. Psalm 119:9-11—How can you remain pure in an impure world? Guard your heart with the Word of God, the Bible.
5. John 8:1-11—Sexual sin is forgivable. Jesus tells the woman to go and sin no more. Secondary virginity is available to those who have fallen and who truly leave their sin behind. Also look at Psalm 51 for a new start.
6. 1 Corinthians 6:18-20—Paul tells us to run away from immorality. You (and your body) were bought with the high price of Jesus' blood. Does your sexual behavior show others how you feel about God?
7. 1 Corinthians 7:1-11—Paul sets high standards. He also says that some may remain single and abstinent for life. Marriage is better than premarital sex. Once you are married, marriage is for life.
8. 2 Corinthians 6:14-16—Choose to date and marry people who share your beliefs.
9. Ephesians 5:1-3 and 5:25-33—Imitate God. Do not practice sexual immorality. Jesus compares the marriage

commitment to His relationship with the Church. He is
the bridegroom; His people are the bride of Christ.

10. Philippians 4:13—"I can do everything through [Christ]
who gives me strength."

11. 1 Thessalonians 4:3-8—Want to know what God's
plan for your life looks like? Read these verses.

12. Hebrews 4:14-16—Jesus was tempted, but did not sin.
He is able to sympathize with our weakness but gives
us His strength to overcome.

- Find a Bible and look up First Corinthians in the New Testament. Start at First Corinthians 6:18 and read to the end
of chapter 7. Did you see anything under a new light?
Write down any notes and/or questions you may have
about this passage.

- Use the Top Twelve Scripture verses to continue looking
up passages in the Bible to shed light on the questions you
may have about sex and relationships.

- Memorize at least one of the Top Twelve Scripture verses
this week.

## Mario and Gina

Mario and Gina have successfully raised three teenagers. In the affluent suburbs where they reside, drinking, drugs and promiscuity mark the teenage culture. Their kids' choices about sex and dating certainly stand out, and as a result, other teens are drawn to their family like a magnet. Each week, forty to fifty high school kids pack into Mario and Gina's home for a Bible study. And you won't hear "Kum Ba Ya" at this meeting; you'll find teens wrestling with a wide range of issues. They are inspired, encouraged and given in-your-face challenges to live a pure life. High standards are explained and expected. So when Mario and Gina's own kids struggle, everyone notices. The strategies and solutions Mario and Gina come up with are noted by many of the other parents in their community.

*You and Mario are regularly asked how you've raised three great teens. What's the secret to raising healthy kids in this fast-lane culture?*

**Gina:** Parenting our three kids is the most awesome thing we've ever done. It takes a tremendous amount of energy and commitment to keep up with what our kids have to face. And when we hit the wall this year with one of our kids, that commitment was put to the test. But when people ask what the secret is, I think they want a quick solution, like a formula for success. It's like anything else; we want a "tip" to fix our golf swing or a diet pill to help us lose twenty pounds. A lot of parents want something like "ten steps to a happy teenager."

## A Secret Weapon

### Clearly, you've found some answers. It may not be a quick fix, but what can parents do better?

**Gina:** There's no doubt that our strength comes from prayer. You might even call it our "secret weapon." Mario and I are on our faces in prayer for our children every day. We consider prayer to be a place to do warfare for our kids. They are in a spiritual battle and prayer is the way that we fight on their behalf.

### When did you begin to pray for your family?

**Gina:** As young parents, our prayer life was just beginning to develop. We would pray every night, "God bless so and so." As the kids grew older, we would pray for events: "Please God, let them win this game, let them get an A in math . . ."—that kind of thing. But as our faith in Christ began to mature, our hearts were more sensitive to the spiritual warfare that our family was facing. Ephesians 6:10-18 talks about putting on the full armor of God. We began to discover that as parents we had to be equipping our family with this armor every day. Mario and I began to pray together, and we found that our relationship grew closer as a result. Prayer was the place for the two of us to communicate with God about the most precious possessions in our lives: our children.

### I know several parents who prayed during tough times in their children's lives. They might say, "I tried prayer, and it didn't work." What would you say to those parents?

**Gina:** Wow, I would certainly sympathize. When your child is going down the wrong path, you want to see God intervene immediately. It is agonizing to watch our children fail and it's natural to blame God. He could fix it, so why doesn't He? Being a parent is a long-term commitment. The joy is in the journey, and prayer is part of the journey. When we look back over the years, we see how God was answering prayers and working for the benefit of our family through the tough times. Trials test your faith and make it more mature; a mature faith increases your patience and endurance.

*That's from James 1:2-4. And speaking of "James," can you tell us about a recent experience where prayer "worked" in your family?*

**Gina:** OK. God has certainly "grown us up" through our son James!

*He's a terrific guy. Good-looking, college athlete, extremely personable. What's the struggle?*

**Gina:** In high school, James began dating a girl from church. We had strong rules about dating: limited alone time, dating only in groups, seeing other girls as well as other friends. These limits make serious dating less likely. But we saw James continually pushing the boundaries. The relationship suffered too. They were moody, fighting a lot, manipulative and secretive. For a while, we insisted that the relationship break up, but they found ways to be together. When James went off to college, the situation was even worse. He was out of our home and free from the restraints. We saw the same problems that he'd faced in high school happening in college. His commitment to grades, sports and other relationships suffered. As his parents, and the people paying for his education, we felt like we needed to take drastic measures and intervene. Of course, we went to prayer to find the answers.

## How did prayer help?

**Gina:** We needed guidance as parents and we desperately needed wisdom. Part of the power of prayer is admitting that you don't have a clue. We looked to other parents for guidance, but not a lot of parents take a stand while their kids are in college. We needed God to speak to us and we needed to listen.

## How does God speak?

**Gina:** When you go to prayer, you pour out your praise, and then you pour out your heart. But then you have to listen. God wants us to hear Him, and He speaks through our hearts, through His Word and through others. We looked for three things in our search for guidance. Most important was Scripture to back us up. We didn't want to make things worse, so we were always looking to find out what God said in the Word. Second, we looked for agreement. Mario and I sometimes see things differently, and when we pray together, we often find ways to agree. Third, we looked for peace. Having a feeling of peace does not mean the strategy will be easier, but it does give you more confidence to carry out the plan you believe is right.

## Where did your journey in prayer lead you?

**Gina:** We gave James a choice. He could continue with the lifestyle he was leading, but he would have to do it without our financial support. That would mean switching to a community college, living at home or getting a job to support himself. For James to stay at his college with our support, he would have to break off the relationship and be more accountable to us.

## *Sounds risky.*

**Gina:** Oh, it was definitely a risk. He could have thumbed his nose at us and done his own thing. But he knew we weren't bluffing and that we were prepared for his answer no matter which way it would go. Giving James this choice was actually a very loving thing to do. It was respectful of his maturity and let him know how committed we are to him and to his future. Teens need strong guidance, even instruction, about dating. We know parents who come down hard about grades, drugs and using the family car, but neglect to give the same attention to the dating issue. I feel we gave James that guidance. As a young adult, he needed to feel the consequences of his choices.

## *And what choice did he make?*

**Gina:** Well, he stayed in school and broke up with the girl. The biggest benefit was in our relationship with him. We're closer now, more trusting of one another. But James will continue to be tested, and believe me, Mario and I are on our knees before God sucking carpet every night for our kids!

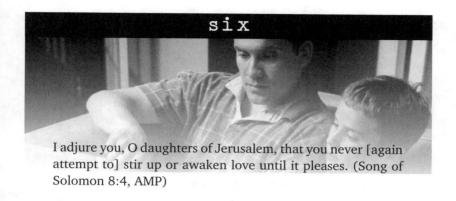

## six

I adjure you, O daughters of Jerusalem, that you never [again attempt to] stir up or awaken love until it pleases. (Song of Solomon 8:4, AMP)

Tragic stories about pregnant eleven-year-olds and fourth-grade pornography addicts should motivate parents to communicate with preteens about sex and its purpose. Through television, children are exposed to sexual language and images, sitcom innuendos and commercials for genital herpes medications. Parents need to educate their children and positively influence their sexual values before TV and the kids at school can negatively influence them.

If you are spending time with your kids and making a connection with them, opportunities will arise for healthy discussion. However, proper timing is crucial. Saying too much too early may introduce ideas prematurely, but if you wait too long you may leave your children ill-prepared for the battles they face in our culture.

The Song of Solomon is a steamy little book in the Old Testament about the courtship and marriage of King Solomon and his beloved. In these eight short chapters, the phrase "I adjure you, O daughters of Jerusalem, do not stir up or awaken love until it pleases," or

# Sex and the Younger Child

something very close to it, is repeated three times (see 2:7; 3:5; 8:4). This verse can be interpreted as saying that it is not good to awaken the senses to sexual questions at too early an age. Opening a discussion on sexuality too early can lead to confusion and experimentation that could be avoided by broaching the subject in the proper way at the proper time.

Schools have begun teaching sex education to younger children with the assumption that it will help to prevent premature sexual activity. Parents must be on guard and be watchful and protective of what their children hear and see.

We need to keep in mind, however, that ignorance is *not* the same as purity. I've actually met a handful of pregnant teens who had no idea how they came to be that way. Ignorance about the facts of life did not ensure their virginity; in fact, a lack of understanding of the basic facts may have left them ill-prepared to handle the sexual situation that led to the pregnancy. Proper information provided in a loving context is the key to equipping your children with both the knowledge and the values to deal with such situations.

Discussing sex with your children is a natural part of parenting, but it must be handled with sensitivity to the age and maturity level of the child. When children ask questions about sex, be sure to answer them as accurately as you can. They have a natural curiosity and if *you* don't give them answers, they will seek them elsewhere. An inquisitive child may ask a series of questions, some of which may be surprising or embarrassing. But giving a concise, caring response is far better than putting him off with, "I'll tell you when you're older."

For some topics, you may want to answer the question with a question in order to clarify what the child is asking. "What's a queer?" will be a tough question to answer without a context. "How did you hear that word?" may be the best first response. (Remember to control your tone of voice. Don't sound as panicked as you feel.) As you find out the context you can more accurately answer the true question. For instance, you may find out that the term *queer* was used to tease a child and therefore you can answer the question with something like, "That is a name other kids use to put you down or make you feel bad."

A quiet child may never ask you about sex. This does not mean he has no interest or questions. Rely on teachable moments to share the story of reproduction. A pregnancy is the most natural visual aid. If you or someone you know is expecting, talk about the developing child and use these discussions as a springboard. Pets can also be a great learning tool. Visit a family with a litter of kittens or pups and let your child see the joy of new life. Saying things like, "I want to answer any questions you have about babies, love and marriage," lets a young child know that you are the person to go to when he has questions.

## Be a Gatekeeper

Innocence is stolen far too soon in our culture. We see five-year-olds imitating a seductively gyrating Britney Spears and seven-year-olds idolizing scantily clad WWF celebrities. Where does this start? It begins at home. Each parent is a gatekeeper to the home. You buy the TV, you pay for the Internet or cable, you rent the movies, you control your children's access to them and you determine the rules. How far do you leave your gate open?

Keep in mind, too, that media may not be the only source of negative influences for your children. Today, children's clothing is often just a child-sized version of the fashions created for the mature adult body. When parents rush to outfit their preschoolers in the latest clothing trends, their kids pick up that value system. They learn that image matters and that perception eclipses character. Rather than joining the forces that hurry our kids into adolescence and rob them of those wonderful years of innocent childhood, be a gatekeeper and set reasonable boundaries for them.

Despite the many influences that bombard your children on a daily basis, you can help to prolong their childhood. Just as we buckle our infants into car seats or keep toddlers from touching a hot stove or a four-year-old from running into a busy street, we must protect our seven- to twelve-year-olds from the dangers of their world. It is a great joy to see an eleven-year-old playing with dolls or a fourteen-year-old who would rather play gladiator with his best friend than go to the mall on a "date." We should encourage our children to stay children, being sure to protect them from harmful outside influences.

How can you be a gatekeeper? Load up your home with classic children's books and videos. Go the extra mile to find clothes that are age-appropriate. Take the TV out of your child's room and closely monitor his access to the Internet. Remember, a well-placed computer in a high-traffic area will help save your children from that chance meeting with Ms. Bimbos from the planet Lesbos.

## Be an Encourager

Your child's body is changing and maturing on its own unique timetable. No one person is just like another. At the moment of conception, all the necessary ingredients that make a unique creature were present. The schedule for growth and development was largely determined at that moment through a one-of-a-kind genetic code. People weren't made with a cookie cutter; each creation is unique and special. The timetable to which your child's body is responding is perfect, planned out in minute detail by our Creator.

You must assure your child of this fact along the way. This principle is most needed during the puberty years when pressures to be thin or rich or cool abound. Tell your child, "Your body is doing just what it was meant to do." What could be more comforting to a slightly pudgy nine-year-old, or to a twelve-year-old with his first real zit? One thirteen-year-old may be singing bass and shaving while his best friend is well under the five-foot mark and looks like a cub scout. One middle school girl plays with Barbies while her locker partner would pass for an adult at the local pub. The growth spurt, the first period, the six-pack (not the beer, the abdominal muscles!), the first bra—all of these things will emerge at the time that is right for each child. When the inner cry of adolescents is to fit in at all costs, the knowledge that there is a greater plan and that their bodies are doing just what they're supposed to may help a child hold the course and weather rough seas.

First Corinthians 6:19 tells us, "Your body is a temple of the Holy Spirit." This means it was designed for holy purposes. God wants our temples to be pure and good and therefore we are to treat our bodies with respect. This concept may help you explain the dangers of molestation and abuse. Without creating unnecessary alarm, simply tell your children that only parents and doctors are allowed to touch them on the area where their bathing suit covers. Tell them that this area is private and personal to them and that there is a "right" kind of touch and a "wrong" kind of touch. Train them to reject any kind of touch that feels "wrong" or "mixed up." Because their body is good and made for good things, you will be affirming that no one should use it for wrong things.

## Give a Gift

I use a simple tool when speaking to fifth-grade girls about the physical changes that happen during adolescence. This illustration can be revisited over and over to open up discussion about growing up and waiting for things to come. It helps kids to identify with the "seven great things your kids need to know" at a level that is younger and more appropriate to their maturity.

The tool is a small box beautifully wrapped with paper and ribbons. I show the box to the kids and then say,

> Let's imagine that someone special in your life has given you a birthday present. "This is your gift," they tell you, "but don't open it until your birthday!" You can't wait to see what's inside of that beautiful box! But there's one problem: Your birthday is still *three weeks* away. Each day you look at that beautiful and mysterious box, wondering what treasure is in store for you. You are so curious that it is getting more and more difficult to wait.
>
> Then, one night, you sneak out of your room and get the box. Very carefully, you slide the ribbons off the package. You then lift the tape at one end, careful not to rip the paper, and pull the box out from the wrapping. You open the box and look inside. Oh! Wow! What a wonderful gift! You can't believe your

eyes! Then you quickly rewrap the gift so no one can tell that it has been opened and hop back into bed before anyone finds out.

Three weeks later, it's your birthday and it's time to open your gift. How do think you would feel? What would you say to the person who gave you the gift?

A lot of kids say they would feel guilty, that their birthday would be ruined and that they would not be surprised because they already knew what was inside the box. I go on to tell the kids,

The gift is you, and the special person who gave you the gift is God. He has wrapped you up in a beautiful package. That wrapping is what people see on the outside of you. Inside is your sexual purity. Your purity, sometimes called virginity, is a wonderful gift. You'll be curious and tempted at times, but don't open the gift. It is a gift you can give to only one person. That one person should be your husband or wife after you get married. That moment is part of the wonderful plan God has for your future and is certainly worth waiting for!

# Zoom in

- What kind of gatekeeper have you been for your kids?
- How will your role as gatekeeper affect your future decisions regarding media, clothing and entertainment choices?
- Tell your child he or she is special and unique. Find qualities that he or she possesses and compliment them.
- Wrap a box and try the gift illustration.

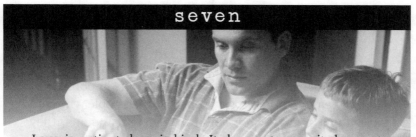

## seven

Love is patient, love is kind. It does not envy, it does not boast, it is not proud. It is not rude, it is not self-seeking, it is not easily angered, it keeps no record of wrongs. Love does not delight in evil but rejoices with the truth. It always protects, always trusts, always hopes, always perseveres. Love never fails. (1 Corinthians 13:4-8)

When we ask teens to wait for sex until marriage, we've given them a destination for their trip. Now they need a road map to get there. The average age for marriage is right around twenty-six[1], so a thirteen-year-old is looking down the road at over ten years of abstinence. From that perspective, it may seem like a life sentence with no hope of parole. As adults, we can offer some guidance as our young people flesh out this goal of remaining pure. The joy is truly in the journey, so we want to provide a successful route to marriage that is full of adventure, excitement and expectation.

One mom asked me what she should say to her ten-year-old daughter about sex. "She wants to know what sex is!" she cried in a panicked voice. "What should I tell her?" I told her to answer the question. Once the "plumbing" lesson is out of they way, kids can begin thinking about the meaning, purpose and intentions of love and sex. When kids are curious about sex, they will continue to ask

# Drawing a Road Map

the people around them until they hear an answer. Pre-teens seeking answers from their peers will hear all sorts of distortions of the truth. That it why it is vitally important for them to hear truthful information from the people who care most about them. When I talk to teenage students, they rarely ask questions about the mechanics of sex. They want to know about relationships. They are asking questions like, "How do I get a boyfriend?"; "How can I say 'no' without hurting her feelings?"; "How do you break up with some-one?".

Ask your children what they are looking for in a relation-ship. Ask them what they think are the qualities or essential ingredients of a good relationship. You may be surprised at their answers. I've asked this question a hundred times and I always hear the same responses: trust, honesty, accep-tance, love, commitment, fun, good communication and re-spect. This seems to be a pretty universal list. I once went to speak to a group of young men in a high security juvenile prison. The boys locked up in that facility had committed horrible crimes and were quite intimidating—they were all dressed in orange prison fatigues and many of them sported gang tattoos. I had no idea how they would re-spond to a message about sexual purity. But, to my sur-prise, when I asked the question "What makes a good relationship?" they listed the same ingredients. No one said good sex, no one said money or cars or a great body. It was their heart's desire to love and be loved.

Once kids identify what is truly important, the "good re-lationship" list becomes a goal. Of course, when kids go looking for relationships, they're not thinking about this list. I've never seen a group of high school girls get excited about how trustworthy a guy is. And boys don't stand around and comment on how well a girl can communicate! No, instead, a different list comes into play. It's the "attraction" list. Looks, clothes, body, popularity, hair, teeth and smile are on this list. It's very superficial, but it is where interest first begins. This feeling of attraction happens quickly. Three to four seconds is all the time most people need. Your kids need to know that the "attraction" list is normal. It's the hook that gets our attention. But they must also understand that attraction and relationship are not the same thing. A boy who has a poster of a supermodel in his room doesn't pretend they have a relationship. He'll soon find that attraction as an end in itself is not very satisfying. His heart is telling him to move from admiration or infatuation toward building strong relationships.

If attraction takes three or four seconds, how long does it take to build a good relationship? Eleven seconds? Most high school students admit that healthy relationships take time. The words on their list imply that time is involved. Trust must be earned, faithfulness must be proven, communication must be established. They admit that this goal should take months or even years to reach. But once we've been hooked by attraction, we don't want to spend a lot of time on this project. We're accustomed to people falling in love and making it to the bedroom in one half-hour TV episode. So teens add physical touch to the mix. They begin to move closer physically and expect that the relationship will just fall into place. They're thinking, *Hey, it worked on TV*.

By the time kids reach high school, they have bought into the notion that if they become closer physically, they will have a good relationship. By asking a few questions about what another couple has "done," they make a determination of the relationship's success. "We did this, this and this,

but not *that*," tells a teenager all he *thinks* he needs to
know. Following this logic, sex will bring a couple closer
and make their relationship better.

At most schools I visit, I see a couple leaning up against
the lockers to make out. I call them the "love couple."
They're all over each other like a cheap suit. At the bell, the
couple practically has to be surgically separated. She kisses
him like he's going to war, and then they watch each other
walk away, one to algebra, the other to Spanish. Onlookers
either turn away in disgust or look on, secretly wishing that
someone would love *them* as passionately. What could be
better than having a boyfriend who would do that?

When I worked for the Crisis Pregnancy Centers, I saw
"love couples" every day. After the pregnancy test, I would
ask them about their relationship. Immediately the girl
would become defensive. "I know my boyfriend loves me,"
she'd begin, "because if he sees me talking to another guy,
he gets really jealous, and that's how I know he loves me."
"I know my girlfriend loves me," the young man would continue. "She calls me ten times a day. She knows my every
move. When I walk in my door, the phone is already ring-
ing, and I know it's her. She comes to all my events, and
when she can't be there, she sends a friend to go instead."
Now, in my world, we call this behavior "stalking," but jealousy, suspicion, doubt and possessiveness seem perfectly
appropriate to the "love couple."

They go on to describe themselves as exclusive and serious. "Exclusive" means they only date each other. Slowly
they begin to ignore their friends, parents, church and
other potential dates. They exclude everyone else and want
more and more time alone. Isolating themselves, their self-
esteem begins to falter. They only feel secure when in each

other's arms. The girl's mood will change based on one word or look from her boyfriend. She has become emotionally dependent on their failing relationship.

*Serious* is a funny word. What does it mean to be serious about a person? It sounds so adult, so forward-thinking. Are they considering marriage? Probably not. I think *serious* is a code word that means "physical." It often means that the "serious" couple is having sex or is very close to it. Because physical involvement is often considered the measure of the success of a relationship, sexual activity with your boyfriend or girlfriend is considered "serious." When the couple goes through tension, they increase the sexual activity as a remedy. They have a relationship but certainly not a very good one. The physical activity which promised intimacy and acceptance has resulted in the exact opposite. Jealousy is the opposite of trust. Commitment, respect and love have all been lost to a counterfeit love affair motivated by lust, selfishness and fear.

What is very sad—even tragic—is that many young people will settle for this jealous, possessive counterfeit. Fear is what motivates the couple to stay together. The only thing worse than the miserable relationship they share would be to break up. Breaking up becomes this couple's greatest fear. "At least I have a girlfriend," I've heard many boys say. "It may not be great, but at least I have something to do on Friday night."

Sex doesn't help them reach the goal of a good relationship. In fact, sex will put things so out of the proper order that the couple may never experience the joy that a healthy friendship could bring. Girls go from boyfriend to boyfriend, giving sex to find love. Boys tend to give "love" to get sex, and both parties are left with a series of heartbreaking scars. This serial monogamy could be preparation for their future divorce. I have heard dating referred to as "divorce practice," and that doesn't seem too far off-base. Without any experience in a healthy, thriving relationship, couples may continue this trend throughout their lives. We must help them understand that building trust, communication, respect and commitment takes time and care. There is no shortcut. *Sex is not a substitute for intimacy.*

*Purity, chastity* and *abstinence* are words we throw around as if they were interchangeable, but they are not. I have met many students who say they are abstaining from sex. When they describe their dating life, however, they could never be described as "pure." Sexual play, oral sex and mutual masturbation are considered "abstinence behaviors" by today's standards. Planned Parenthood's abstinence brochure provides a detailed description of "outercourse" activities like erotic massage and body rubbing to achieve orgasm without actual intercourse.

Kids learn to view intercourse as the only boundary. They begin to cruise the edge, doing everything else you can imagine and calling it purity. I call it technical virginity. Poor relationships, oral diseases and trashed reputations are the rewards of technical virginity. And a technical virgin doesn't stay one for very long. If we desire sexual purity for our children, we must address the big question: "How far can I go?"

I like to show students a quarter that I found clinking around in my dryer. It had fallen out of someone's pocket, and in our house it's finders keepers when it comes to money in the laundry. The reason I was interested in this particular quarter was its year: 1976. Right away I recognized the special edition coin with the 1776-1976 bicentennial emblem on the reverse. You see, I had a quarter just like this one up in my drawer of favorite things.

Back in 1976 I visited the U.S. Mint where they were making thousands of these special commemorative quarters. After the tour, I bought one for twenty-five cents. But the quarter I bought at the mint was packaged and sealed in a plastic case. It had never been opened, never spent, never touched by a human hand. Well, that quarter has become pretty valuable over the years. If you collect anything or if you've ever watched the *Antiques Road Show*, you know that things increase in value based on beauty, condition and rarity. So my mint-condition quarter is worth far more than the original amount I paid for it. But the one I pulled from the dryer? It's worth twenty-five cents.

Teens treat their great gift of virginity like that quarter I found in the dryer. They let people touch it, spend it and use it. Rather than gaining in value, it becomes worn, common and cheap. The sealed coin is beautiful, valuable and rare, just like sexual virginity.

When kids ask, "How far can I go?" find out what it is they want to know. Are they merely asking how much they can get away with—how far can they go and not get pregnant? Look deeper and you may find it is a search for rules and steps on which they can base good decisions as they begin the dating process in search of a mate. There certainly are limits a parent can set. The Bible is clear on the limits of sexual intercourse and can therefore be an excellent guide for you as you set your own limits.

It will be tempting to draw a line for them, saying, "You can do this and this, but not that." I used to suggest that kids not kiss outside the circle they could draw around their face. I quickly found that even that conservative suggestion was too far for some young teens to go.

Purity involves more than simply drawing a line that you won't cross. It is an ever-increasing desire to do what is right. Teach your kids to think about the goal: Is this activity increasing communication? Are we building trust? Are we having fun or is this getting too serious? Instead of asking, "How far can I go?" teach them to ask, "How much can I save for marriage?" and "How far can I go to please God?" And ask yourself, "How far would I go as a parent to help my child protect this precious gift?"

## What Are the Rules?

It is very appropriate to give strong guidelines about how to behave with the opposite sex. A book called *The Rules* by Ellen Fein and Sherrie Schneider became an overnight bestseller in the late 1990s not because of its self-seeking "how to get a man" strategies but because it gave women rules. After years of losing in the sex game, women were looking for clear-cut strategies for success in relationships. Today's teens also want to know how to play to win and they are looking to us to tell them. Good manners, etiquette rules, when to hold hands, when to kiss, how to break up—these were all clearly communicated to the youth of yesteryear through family and community. Also, training movies such as *Are You Popular?*, *How Much Affection?*, *What to Do on a Date?* and *Dating Do's and Don'ts* that taught these standards were common throughout the 1950s and '60s.[2]

Today those rules are a nostalgic memory, one of the casualties of the feminist movement. Men who desire to hold doors, act honorably and protect the innocent may be called "chauvinists." And well-mannered teens are portrayed as hung up, weird or gay. I don't mean that kids should act like Eddie Haskell ("Good morning, Mrs. Cleaver. May Wallace come down to join the fellows?"), but basic rules about social behavior give kids much-needed confidence in tough situations. Later on in this book, you'll read some specific rules about dating that were suggested by real parents that may help you in establishing rules for your own children. Remember that it is also important that you establish the *reasons* for the high standards that you set. Your child is valuable; that's why saving sex is so important.

I was speaking to a group of teens one night about setting rules and standards for dating. One boy seemed to stare right through me. He looked out of place in the small church youth group in his postmodern uniform of giant pants, purple hair and multiple body piercings. After the talk, he waited in line to speak with me. He was kind of scary and I wanted to head for the door, but to my surprise he told me of his current courtship with a tenderness that defied his appearance. "I really liked this girl," he said, "but she told me she was not allowed to date until she was sixteen. Her parents were really strict about that point. I waited a whole year and got to know her at school as a friend. Then, on her sixteenth birthday, I called her house and her dad answered the phone. 'You want to take out my daughter don't you, son?'

"I freaked. But I said, 'Yes, sir. I've waited a year, and I'd like to go out with her.'

" 'Well,' her dad said, 'I want you to know she's the most precious thing in my life, but if you are willing to follow the rules, you can come on over. She's waiting for you.' "

That young man felt like he'd won the lottery. He knew he was taking out someone valuable, special and prized. After five months of dating, he's never even kissed her. He smiled as he whispered, "I'm waiting until I know it's right, and I might be waiting a long time."

## Zoom in

- Discuss with your child the qualities of a good relationship.

- Identify the difference between attraction and relationship.

- Think of ways to increase trust, honesty, communication and respect. Does today's dating culture encourage those qualities?

- If your child asks, "How far can I go?" how will you respond?

## Notes:

1. National Center for Policy and Analysis. Available from: <http://www.ncpa.org/pd/social/social2.html>.
2. Ken Smith, *Mental Hygiene: Better Living Through Classroom Films* (Blast Books, 1945-1970). The videos are available from <http://www.archive.org/movies/movies.php>.

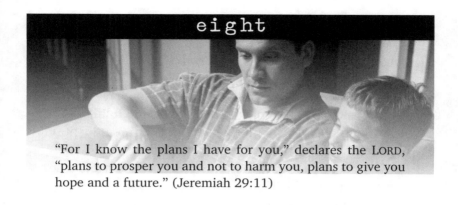

## eight

"For I know the plans I have for you," declares the LORD, "plans to prosper you and not to harm you, plans to give you hope and a future." (Jeremiah 29:11)

*he Princess Diaries* is the story of how an awkward teenager's life is changed when she finds out she is heir to the throne of a small country. Even though she is the rightful princess, it is young Mia's decision whether or not to rule. Her grandmother, the queen, encourages Mia to step up and accept a destiny that only she can fulfill. Over the next two weeks, "princess lessons" and a dramatic makeover transform Mia's appearance, but a change of heart must also take place before she takes the throne. The reality sinks in as she reads a letter from her father. "From now on," he states, "You'll be·traveling the road between who you think you are and who you can be. The key is to allow yourself to make the journey." Mia has always been royal; now she has the opportunity to act on that fact.

First Peter 2:9 says, "You are a chosen people, a royal priesthood, a holy nation, a people belonging to God." Romans 8:14-17 explains that our relationship to God is one of sonship: We are full heirs to the kingdom of God. Through faith in Christ, your sons and daughters, and you too, are royalty; the very children of the King of

## Fulfilling a Destiny

kings. Consider what this means: You can take hold of all of heaven's riches in the name of your Father. Your inheritance is secure, sealed by the Holy Spirit. You have a royal identity and God has a plan that only you can fulfill.

Instilling our teens with that sense of purpose, identity and destiny gives them a reason to hold to higher standards, to act on the fact that they possess a great purpose that is yet to unfold. Their choices about speech, clothing, attitude and relationships begin to reflect a "royal" identity.

A young woman who has done some speaking for me tells of her successful journey out of poverty and hopelessness because of the strong sense of identity communicated to her by her parents. "They always told me I was special," she recalls, "and that I was going to be somebody! I began acting as if I were somebody special and making decisions to make that a reality." Lisa Beamer, wife of Flight 93 hero Todd Beamer, addressed a middle school memorial service commemorating the September 11 tragedy that took her husband's life. "Be the person you want to become," she encouraged. "A hero doesn't wait for someday; a hero begins to live his dream today." Many teens wait for someday. They think, "Someday I'll get married and be faithful. Someday I'll treat others well. Someday I'll live a pure life." We must encourage them that "someday" is here and now.

One of my favorite books is *Ben-Hur*. (The movie was OK, but you've got to read the book to get beyond the whole chariot race thing.) It is the story of a young man born at the time of Christ who is trying to find his way in the world after the death of his father. In an early scene, we find Ben-Hur at age fourteen lounging on the couch with his head in his mother's lap. On the cusp of manhood, this tender moment is probably the last time he will linger in his mother's embrace. As she looks down into his face, he asks, "Mother, what will I become?" This is a question that most children ask, in their own way. To answer the longings in our children's hearts, we could respond to this question in many ways. Ben-Hur's mother could have promised him a job in commerce like his father, or a position in the growing army of Rome. He could have studied at the temple, or joined his uncle in foreign trade.

But she doesn't talk of career, or future or what will be possible. Instead she tells young Ben-Hur the familiar story of his forefathers and his forefathers' God. She tells him about how God led them out of Egypt to a new land of promise. She tells him of the judges, kings and battles. She reminds him of the heritage that melts race, family and faith into a galvanized identity. She doesn't tell him what he will be; she tells him *who he is.*

Within the next twenty-four hours, a fluke accident will turn Ben-Hur's life upside down and take him on a journey from the depths of prison life to the heights of Roman aristocracy. It is not these circumstances, but his strong sense of identity and purpose that finally lead this young prince to his ultimate destiny.

Your child's destiny is not just a destination. It's more like a cross-country road trip. The ultimate destination is determined by the journey. If you take a detour, the destination is delayed. Make a wrong turn early in the trip and you may never even reach the goal. That is why our decisions about dating are so crucial in the early years of adolescence. The great author C.S. Lewis said it this way:

> Good and evil both increase at compound interest.
> That is why the little decisions you and I make every
> day are of such infinite importance. The smallest

good act today is the capture of a strategic point from which, a few months later, you may be able to go on to victories you never dreamed of.[1]

A girl chooses her clothing, style of music, movies and friends. These little decisions influence bigger decisions about sex and her choice of a mate. A young man who decides to do the right thing, to not cheat when cheating would be easy, to not look at a *Playboy*, to control himself with strength and integrity, will be likely to make wise decisions as an adult. Encourage your kids to be the people they want to become. He who is faithful in the little things will be given responsibility for much more (see Matthew 25:21).

My dad is our family historian. He and my aunt have spent countless hours researching the family line back to the early 1600s. When I show my kids this enormous tree of names and dates, it illustrates the relationship we have to a family of the past, present and future. It is helpful, too, to point out that some of these people were truly "great, great" folks, and some of them were not so great. The choices of those old folks, good and bad, still have impact today. Likewise the choices my children make now will someday be scrutinized by future generations. Among the letters discovered in the family research was one from my grandfather to his young son that tenderly instilled value and vision.

My dear son,

Twenty-one years ago on the eighth of May in the County of Montgomery, State of Georgia, you were born. Therefore, when that date arrives, you will have become a citizen with all the privileges and responsibilities that citizenship carries and implies.

I want you to know that you have been a good boy and a credit to your mother and to me, who is proud indeed to be your father.

You would do well to remember that honesty is the best policy, that virtue is its own reward, that honor and shame from no condition rise, act well your part, there all the honor lies.

With gratitude to Divine Providence for you, and love and affection toward you, I remain,

Your faithful and obedient servant.

You don't really know what your child will ultimately become, but you have much to do with shaping his future. Consider writing a letter or giving a significant token or heirloom to each of your children. Wrap the gift in ceremony and meaning. Let them know who they are and where they are going. What is your hope for them? What vision do you instill? Lasting love, a happy marriage, a peaceful and productive life? These are the marks of a person of destiny and purpose.

- How do you build a sense of identity, purpose and destiny in your kids' lives?

- Think of ways to show your sons and daughters who they are, using photos, a family tree, reunions, etc.

- Tell your children that they have a purpose and a destiny that only they can fulfill.

- Ask them how other people would recognize them as "royalty."

- Do their clothing, speech and choice of friends reflect a royal identity? Ask them why or why not?

## What's Your Vision?

I once met with a teenage couple, the proud parents of adorable twin girls. Both only eighteen years old, this couple had been living together for almost two years. A surprise pregnancy changed everything, and now they were new parents facing an uncertain future. "When do you think you might get married?" I asked them. It seemed like a natural next step to me. After all, they were living together and had children. I'll never forget their answer: "Marriage is for the old people at Denny's," the new mom responded. "By the time my babies grow up, those people will all be dead." Isn't it chilling to think that the next generation sees marriage as obsolete? (Not to mention that I kind of like Denny's!) She continued to explain, "You grew up with a vision of a white dress, a long aisle and heart-shaped bathtubs in the Poconos—happily-ever-after stuff. But that's *your* dream, not mine."

Both of these young people came from broken families. So, for these kids, marriage may have seemed like an impossible dream, a worn-out institution seen only in black-and-white TV reruns. As a result, they dismissed marriage and were ready to try anything else that promises love and comfort. They simply did not have a vision for marriage.

Traditionally, weddings were community events where all generations gathered to celebrate the birth of a new family. Today's weddings, however, are becoming less and less traditional. Receptions have become expensive, sometimes extravagant affairs where seating is limited and children are not always welcome. In fact, many young people have never even been to a wedding ceremony. I asked a classroom of eleven-year-old girls how many of them had ever been to a wedding: Only three hands went up. These three had each attended their own mother's wedding to their stepdad. The rest had seen marriage ceremonies only on TV.

If we take our cues from *Bride* magazine, weddings become no more than photo events, much like the prom or graduation. Talk to most engaged couples and you'll find that they are not planning their marriage; they are planning a wedding. Choosing the color of the napkins takes days, while looking over the vows is done in seconds.

No wonder we have a generation choosing cohabitation instead of marriage! Living together looks much simpler than all the hoopla surrounding marriage. Rutgers' National Marriage Project released a recent report on the top ten reasons young men won't marry. David Popenoe, the project's codirector, says that half of all first marriages are now being preceded by living together. Guys can postpone marriage indefinitely, with all the benefits of a quasi-wife. They can get sex without marriage. They want to avoid divorce and its financial risks and fear that marriage will require too many changes and compromises.

"The problem is that men just don't realize what's in it for them," says Atlanta psychiatrist Frank Pittman. Author of the book *Grow Up!*, he says we have not done a good job of selling marriage to men.

> They don't know all the good things that will change their lives. Married men are healthier than single men, wealthier, they live longer and happier lives, they have more sex. And they have somebody who knows them and tolerates them anyway.[2]

If we are going to ask our kids to wait for marriage to have sex, then marriage better be something highly prized, something permanent, something worth waiting for. We've got to give them a vision. You can build a realistic expectation about marriage by attending weddings with your kids (often they can attend the ceremony even if they weren't invited to the reception), talking about what makes a successful marriage and pointing to qualities and character traits in people that help to build strong relationships.

Four years after my initial meeting with that young couple that was living together, I saw the twins' mother once again. She had been to a family reunion celebrating her grandparents' fiftieth wedding anniversary. She shared with me her recaptured dream: "I *do* want to get married someday," she admitted. "I want my children to be able to see my husband and me together after fifty years of marriage." Something about the party had planted a vision in that young woman's mind. In one evening, a dream was restored, a hope renewed. Her deep, unquenchable desire is the same as yours and mine: to love and be loved for a lifetime. All it took was someone to tell her that the vision could be a reality.

## Dare to Dream

Let me plant a vision in your mind:

> It is your daughter's wedding day. You stand with her at the back of the church, waiting for the familiar wedding march to begin. All your friends and family have come to celebrate with you. Your future son-in-law is a wonderful young man and someone you would have hand-picked to join your family. Your daughter is wearing a beautiful white dress, and around her neck is the heart-shaped locket you gave her as a young teen. Inside is the tiny reminder of a promise she made to remain pure. She's all grown up now, but you see in her face the little girl you nurtured and held in your arms. She gently takes your

hand and through her tears she confides in you, "To-night will be our first night together as man and wife. Thanks to you, we waited!"

It's moving day for your son. It's his first apartment. He's got a promising job, a reliable car and now a place of his own. Where did the time go? For a moment the mix of joy and loss builds a knot in your throat and tears sting your eyes. You carry a box of dishes into the small kitchen and see a young lady putting things into the cupboards. As you introduce yourself, the thought *Roommate?* is going through your mind. Your son takes the heavy box from your arms and pulls you aside. "Jen's here helping me out today. She's a great girl. Her parents are like you—really strong morals, you know. Don't worry: Even if things do get serious, we've both already committed to waiting for sex."

Are you dreaming? Yes. You *should* dream for your children. You should have a bright vision for their future relationships and tell them often of your dreams for them. *Sexual abstinence until marriage is a reasonable, attainable and desirable goal.* Do you believe that? Is it possible in today's culture to raise children who will make wise and honorable decisions about sex? It's not only possible, it's a growing trend. Students choosing to wait for sex are once again in the majority. More than half of all high school students have never had sex. And over 1 million teens have signed a contract called True Love Waits, a pledge to wait for sex until marriage. Maintaining a high standard may not be the easy road, but it is a road that is getting more traffic lately.

# Notes:

1. C.S. Lewis, *Mere Christianity* (New York: Simon & Schuster, 1980), Book 9, p. 117.
2. Frank Pittman, *Grow Up! How Taking Responsibility Can Make You a Happy Adult* (New York: St. Martin's Press, 1999), p. 158.

## nine

Two are better than one, because they have a good return for their work: If one falls down, his friend can help him up. But pity the man who falls and has no one to help him up! Also, if two lie down together, they will keep warm. But how can one keep warm alone? Though one may be overpowered, two can defend themselves. A cord of three strands is not quickly broken. (Ecclesiastes 4:9-12)

Each summer, I attend three or four weddings. Each one is special. Some include a moving sermon, some are breathtakingly beautiful, with string quartets and mounds of roses, candles and flowing taffeta. But the element of the service I tune in to is the vows. They really are the main event. Everything else is window dressing. Writing your own vows is popular right now. The couple chooses their own words or poetry to make the promises of marriage. The parents cry, the teenagers sigh and the flower girl fidgets in her itchy new dress. This is great so long as the essential vows are being communicated. At one wedding, I never heard the words "obey," "faithful" or " 'til death do us part" or anything that indicated a lifelong commitment. *If either one wants to get out of this contract*, I thought, *they've got a major loophole.* No promises had actually been spoken.

What are the vows of marriage? The standard Christian wedding vows as we know them today can be traced back to the Mid-

# Marriage Is for Keeps

dle Ages. Marriage in any culture includes the same general ingredients. *The Prayerbook of Edward VI*, who reigned in England from 1537-1553, includes this marriage ceremony that, with a few language updates, is still widely used today.

> Dearly beloved friends, we are gathered together here in the sight of God and in the face of His congregation to join this man and this woman in a holy matrimony, which is an honorable estate instituted of God in paradise, signifying unto us the mystical union that is betwixt Christ and His Church: Which holy estate, Christ adorned and beautified with His presence, and first miracle that He wrought in Cana of Galilee, and is commended of Saint Paul to be honorable among all men; and is therefore not to be enterprised, nor taken in hand unadvisedly, lightly or wantonly to satisfy men's carnal lusts and appetites like brute beasts that have no understanding: but reverently, discretely, advisedly, soberly and in the fear of God.

Once having these and other preliminary statements clearly stated, the man and his betrothed are asked to make these vows:

> Wilte thou have this woman to be thy wedded wife, to live together after God's own ordinance in the holy estate of matrimony? Wilte thou love her, comfort her, honor and keep her in sickness and in health? And forsaking all others, keep thee only to her, so long as you both shall live? *The man shall answer.* I will.
>
> Wilte thou have this man to be thy wedded husband, to live together after God's own ordinance in the holy estate of matrimony? Wilte thou obey him, and serve him, love, honor and keep him in sickness and in health? And forsaking all others, keep thee only to

him, so long as you both shall live? *The woman shall answer.* I will.

And the minister, receiving the woman at her father or friends' hands, shall cause the man to take the woman by the right hand and so either give their troth to each other, the man first saying:

I [N.] take thee [N.] to my wedded wife, to have and to hold from this day forward, for better, for worse, for richer, for poorer, in sickness, and in health, to love and to cherish, til death us depart; according to God's holy ordinance: And thereto I plight thee my troth.

With this ring I thee wed: This gold and silver I give thee: with my body I worship thee: and with all my worldly goods I thee endow. In the name of the Father, and of the Son, and of the Holy Ghost. Amen.[1]

Even with the "thees" and "thous," there is no question that this couple is married! Note the interesting language used to illustrate the bonds of marriage. To "plight [your] troth" means to weave two truths together. According to the *Merriam-Webster Collegiate Dictionary,* to "ply" is to fold, braid or weave layers of fabric into one stronger material. *Troth* is an old term meaning "truth." Imagine weaving all that is truly yourself forever with all of your beloved's true self. To weave your truths together is more than just giving your word. The picture is one of strength that is built on trust.

During the wedding ceremony, the couple is reminded of the mystical union between Christ and His Church. Marriage is a solemn covenant or promise. God takes promises very seriously. His promises to the Church have been blood covenants, sealed in precious blood. Under the old covenant, the promise was made through the blood of perfect lambs and other animals sacrificed on the altar. Christ's own sinless blood, spilled for us, is the new covenant that allows us access to God. The promise of marriage is made in blood as well: When the virgin bride's hymen is broken upon first intercourse, she sheds a small amount of blood. This beautiful picture of a promise sealed in blood is still part of God's desire for marriages today.

Throughout the Middle Ages, the couple's right hands were sometimes symbolically tied together during the ceremony to signify the yoke of marriage. The "weds" were the pledges that the future husband gave to his bride-to-be. The "weds" were sealed with the tying of the hands, much like two oxen would be tied to a yoke.[2] It's where we get sayings like "tying the knot" or "getting hitched." The yoking of two people infers that there is difficult work ahead—hard ground that will need to be turned, tilled and planted. The joy is knowing that someone is beside you to help ease that load and share in the fruit of the labor. The knot is tied in all circumstances: for richer, for poorer, in sickness and in health, until death separates us.

## Marriage Is Forever

Part of the instruction that we should be giving our kids about marriage is the vision of love that lasts a lifetime. My friend and pastor, Ted Martin, illustrates this notion of living and loving, a lesson he learned from his grandparents, affectionately known as PaPa and GeeMa. I'll let him tell the story.

> My grandparents were married for over fifty years. Both artistic and passionate people, they would sometimes really get into it. Arguments were not unusual, but then they'd love each other just as passionately and deal with their differences. It was fun to watch, and through the

years they became a model to me of how to live and how
to love. In the last twelve years of their marriage, PaPa
became a nurse to GeeMa, who had suffered a major
stroke. On a daily basis, my PaPa was dealing with his
wife as she was steadily declining. Slowly her body was
failing, both mentally and physically. She was unable to
do all the things that were once so easy. Unable to take
care of her husband or herself, she was dealing with the
frustration of her body not responding the way it should.
And all the while, there was PaPa, ministering to her,
serving her, loving her.

As things progressively got worse, GeeMa had to move
into her own room and into her own bed. Speaking became more and more difficult for her, so from her bed
she would blow a little whistle whenever she had a need.
PaPa would come in and get a glass of water for her, help
her use the bathroom or help her sit upright. Later, she
became so weak that she couldn't blow the whistle any
longer and she used a small bell. And in the middle of the
night, PaPa would hear the bell and get up, walk into
GeeMa's room and tend to her needs, then go back to his
bed. Dawn no longer signaled the start of a new day, because his day never really ended. It was a continuous service of waking with the bell, sleeping when he could,
pouring out his life for the sake of his wife, seeking to
minister to her needs and recognizing what it means to
live and to love.

Well, this one time, the bell rang again. PaPa could
have very easily rolled over and put the pillow over his
ears and said, "I am just too tired; this is enough. I'm just
going to sleep though it this time." But he didn't. He got
up out of bed and dutifully walked to GeeMa's room. She
motioned to him to help her up, so he lifted her to sit on
the bed. She motioned to him again, her gesture saying,
"Get me to my feet." So he picked her all the way up and

enabled her to stand on her feet. She stood there and looked into PaPa's weary, tired eyes and said, "Carl, I love you," she said, "And I have always loved you." And then she died right there in his arms.

For better, for worse, for richer, for poorer, in sickness and in health. Love for a lifetime.

- Write a short vision statement for each of your children.

- Think about that vision and picture the people who will be the future spouses of your children. Pray for those young people who will someday be part of your family.

- Read the wedding vows found earlier in this chapter (page 88) to your children. Use real-life couples that you know to illustrate to them richer and poorer, sickness and health, better and worse situations that test the bonds of marriage.

- Encourage your child to think about the kind of person he wants to marry someday. Ask him to write down the qualities he is looking for.

- Do you believe abstinence until marriage is possible for your own children? Why or why not? What particular obstacles are standing in the way of your children maintaining sexual purity?

## Notes:

1. Vows taken from *The Prayerbook of Edward VI*, available on-line from: <http://library.byu.edu/~rdh/eurodocs/uk/weded.html>.
2. Sharon L. Krossa, "Historical Handfasting" [on-line], April 5, 2002. May 8, 2003. Available from: <http://www.medievalscotland.org/history/handfasting.shtml>.

## Charles and Rita

Charles and Rita Rodgers have four kids, three of whom have graduated from high school. "Sometimes we wonder if all we've said to our kids really sinks in," Rita told me. After hearing the following story, I know it did.

**Rita:** As we stood waving good-bye to our daughter at her dorm room steps, we were already beginning to wonder how Jen would handle the pressures of college life. "We've raised her with high standards," we reassured each other. "She knows right from wrong." But would she be able to resist the alcohol, the partying and the attention of college men? Just weeks later, we received a letter. *Wow, she needs money already*, we thought. But the tender letter revealed a heart committed to purity.

Dear Mom and Dad,

Thank you. You can't believe what goes on here. There are plenty of temptations that would take me away from the things you taught us at home, but so far I have been able to stand up for what I believe. My new friends here ask me about my values; I know they respect me. Thanks for preparing me for this.

Love, Jen

The next letter came three months later:

Dear Mom and Dad,

I met a guy. His name is Sam and he's wonderful. We've decided to take it slowly and get to know each other as friends. He's never even kissed me, but I feel so close to him. Everyone says we're nuts, but I think they all know that we have something special. I can't wait for you to meet him!

Love, Jen

## Ready for College?

Two years later, Sam shyly asked Charles if he could have permission to marry Jen. The bride will be wearing white.

### Jen says you prepared her for this. How did you do that?

**Rita:** We're not really sure! Her decision to "court" instead of date was kind of a surprise to us. We had encouraged the kids to remain pure for their future husband or wife, so I guess that it stems from that. I think that kids see things as black and white. There seemed to be no middle ground for Jen on this issue. She chose to wait for marriage, and that included waiting for everything.

Charles and I had established a curfew for our kids and we handled decisions about dating and phone calls as those things came up. We took time to get to know our kids' friends and that really paid off. We found that the kids came to our house instead of going out. Maybe it was cheaper, but whatever the reason, it continues today. When the kids and their friends are home from college, everyone gathers here. It's great. These relationships began with involvement at the youth group at church, and that was a great support. Finding people who support your values is crucial.

**Charles:** We also made it clear to the kids that we expected the best from them. But we aren't overbearing, just reasonable.

### Are you ready to walk Jen down the isle?

**Charles:** Wow, I know I'm going to lose it. What a mixture of sadness and joy! It's a wonderful beginning. And I know that Jen and Sam are going to make it through to the end.

## ten

These commandments that I give you today are to be upon your hearts. Impress them on your children. Talk about them when you sit at home and when you walk along the road, when you lie down and when you get up. Tie them as symbols on your hands and bind them on your foreheads. Write them on the doorframes of your houses and on your gates. (Deuteronomy 6:6-9)

"It's 11 o'clock: Do you know where your children are?" Some of you may remember this slogan from a 1970s campaign encouraging parents to reconnect with their kids. Let me ask you a new-millennium question: "It's 11 o'clock: Do you know *who* your children are?" I once heard author and speaker Josh McDowell say to an audience of parents, "Rules without relationship equals rebellion." I agree and would make a corollary statement as well: "Relationship without rules equals confusion." How do you balance rules and relationship? Can you expect obedience to appropriate rules while maintaining a healthy parent/child relationship through the adolescent years? Our Reality Parenting contributors all say, "Yes, you can," and they all agree that there are three commitments that help make it all work. The first of these commitments is spending time.

# Building Relationships

# Spending Time

Our family visited a local science museum this past summer. The place was packed with summer camp kids and vacationing families. Early in the day I spotted a five- or six-year-old boy darting from display to display, stopping at each to turn and look back into his father's face. *How sweet,* I thought, *a father and son out for some quality time.* The dad was following his son and was talking as he walked along, but he did not appear to be talking to his son. When I looked more closely, I saw that he was wearing a headset and was talking on the phone. When we saw the two later in the day, the boy was sitting on the floor staring deep into the carpet. His dad stood at his side but was a million miles away, still talking on the phone.

The idea of "quality time" emerged in the 1980s when more and more moms went to work outside the home. Between work, school, sports, meetings and housework, many families found time to be their most limited resource. Shrinking most rapidly was time spent at home with the kids, so the notion of *quality* rather than *quantity* time became a comforting remedy. The problem with quality time in my home is that my window of quality time doesn't always fit with my kids' schedules. When I meet my daughter at the bus stop, she is already talking on the way down the bus steps. During the short walk home I hear every detail, every heartbreak, every victory from the day's events. I listen, she talks. A hug and a snack usually solve all of the problems of the day.

My son, who shares the same two parents and was raised in the same home, bears no resemblance to my daughter in his after-school "ritual" (except for the snack part). I ask, "How was your day?" I get, "I dunno, what do we have to eat?" Four o'clock in the afternoon is not his quality time. Later, around 11:30 p.m., when I'm in a relative coma, he is ready to talk. But if I stay awake and sit and listen and laugh and chat, I'll hear about his struggles, his dreams, his questions and his fears. I've found that this window of opportunity is the most effective time to give direction about sexual issues. Trust is gradually established and opens the door for rules and guidelines. Is it worth the quantity of time I have to carve out of the day? You know it is.

It's not just taking time to be with your kids that matters, but making sure there is face-to-face time where communication has an opportunity to grow. Many parents have complained that their teenage children simply will not talk to them. They become frustrated by one-word answers and shrugs that are the only communication they receive. Spending time does not always mean there will be conversation, but it does mean you are creating a place for it to happen. There are times when simply doing something together will be valuable. Give your growing child your full attention—be affectionate and encouraging.

Appropriate affection communicates love and warmth when words can't. Just being available to spend time with your child is the important part. Kids who do not find ways to express their feelings at home will look elsewhere. Teens, especially girls, will often find affection in the arms of a stranger if it is not found at home. "Hands-on" parenting has been proven to keep kids away from drugs, smoking and promiscuity. So hug your child often, take him along on your errands, join him in his room to listen to the radio—find ways to be there. But, as we learned from the man at the science museum, spending time is more than just being present. We must seek the kinds of activities that help to build the lines of communication. That leads us to the second commitment: choosing *active* rather than *passive* entertainment to build relationships.

- Honestly gauge how much time you spend with each of your children. Be specific. How many minutes a day?

- How much communication is going on? Gauge from 1-10.

- Do your children confide in you? When and where?

- How is your level of affection with your children? Is it on the rise or on the decline?

- Ask some of the open-ended questions you worked on in the previous chapter.

- Make a commitment to carve out more "face" time this week. Again, be specific and deliberate about how you will reach your goal.

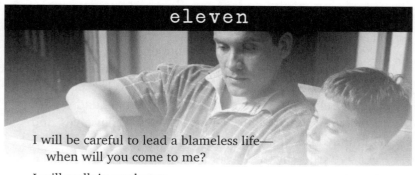

## eleven

I will be careful to lead a blameless life—
   when will you come to me?

I will walk in my house
   with blameless heart.
I will set before my eyes
   no vile thing. (Psalm 101:2-3)

The most popular date in America is going to the movies. On hundreds of occasions I have told students that if they want to build a relationship with someone, a movie is the worst possible date idea. You sit in a dark room with no eye contact where you have to be quiet and see something you probably have to (or should) censor. Afterward, the conversation remains fairly one-dimensional: Question, "What did you think of the movie?" Reply, "It was OK. Where do you want to eat?"

Teenagers don't develop this habit of going to the movies by accident. As children, they were taken out on "dates" or family outings. Where did their parents take them? To the movies, of course. They have learned that "going out" means going to a movie. Movies, watching TV and videos and playing computer games are all ways that we are technically "spending time," but these activities teach us very little about our kids and teach them very little about us. To-

## Active Entertainment Choices

day's standards for family entertainment have become increasingly passive, and as kids grow up their dating patterns will tend to be the same way. We are not truly building relationships during this passive time, and we are not showing our children how to share themselves and communicate with others.

A 1999 study by the Kaiser Family Foundation revealed some alarming statistics about just how passive our entertainment has become. The typical American child, age eight and up, spends thirty-eight hours each week consuming media outside of the school day. Four hours each day is spent watching TV. Sixty-one percent of those kids said there were no parental rules about TV viewing and that the TV was on during mealtime.

The study also found that teens report that TV is their primary source of information about sex. In fact, parents are joining their kids to watch TV only five percent of the time. We allow TV, computers and game boxes to rob us of valuable time when we could be relating to our kids. Family time around the dinner table is considered by most family counselors to be the single most important connection point of the week, yet most American mealtimes are misspent in front of a glowing screen.[1]

But what can young people do instead of watching TV or going to a movie? When I ask teens this question, I hear crickets. In other words, they stare at me with blank faces and then complain that there's nothing to do in their town. Sometimes giving them a few guidelines can help to get their heads into gear. I ask them to generate a list of activities that can be done during the day, are not too expensive and can be done with a group. With those qualifiers in mind, they can usually come up with a pretty good list of alternatives to the movie date. Skating, washing the car, cooking dinner, making crafts, biking or hiking are all activities that become much more fun when shared with a friend or parent. By following these criteria, dating is redefined and becomes much more interactive and fun.

So turn off the TV and pick up a hobby or interest that involves your son or daughter. Doing a puzzle or playing a board game requires more cooperation and can be more interactive than a video game. The more active the entertainment choice, the better. Your child will not only learn more about you, he'll have a great model for building relationships through the teen years and you'll lay a foundation for our third commitment: setting reasonable rules.

## Zoom in

- Generate a list of at least ten active entertainment choices that are realistic for your family. Choose activities that can be done as a family or in pairs with parent and child.
- List ideas for all seasons.
- Keep the list in a highly visible place.
- Commit yourself to doing something with your family from your list this week.
- Schedule creative "dates" with your children on a regular basis and stick to them.

(Note: Building relationships should not drain the family finances, so be careful to make sure that the plans are not too extravagant or expensive. Simple is good. Even play-

ing a new board game together can be a relationship-
builder.)

## Note:

1. Bob DeMoss's book, *Learn to Discern*, now a family classic, exposes this
   media monster and gives practical suggestions to tame the beast in the
   box.

## Jim and Mollie

Jim and Mollie like technology. Jim teaches middle school math and Mollie is a doctor with a busy travel schedule. They have two children in their early teens. Jim and Mollie depend on the latest gadgets to keep their relationships connected and their schedules coordinated throughout the week. Cell phones, digital date books and the Internet are a way of life. But these tools have a downside. Jim and Mollie recently found that sometimes convenience isn't worth the price.

**Jim:** Our daughter, Kit, discovered instant-messaging programs and chat rooms last year. These programs seem great at first. Kids can communicate with each other in real time with no phone bills. Kit had a buddy list of kids she knew from church and school. It seemed like such a wonderful convenience: She could talk to all of her friends without tying up the phone. However, over the next few months, we found that the kids were glued to this thing. Home-work, chores and family time were being subverted by the Internet.

### *Were there any restrictions or limits?*

**Jim:** Sure. We set time limits, had the computer placed in a central location and had filtering software to help ensure that they weren't getting into anything they shouldn't. We really thought that these things would work. But, you can get lost on the Internet. Time just slips away. That goes for games, chat rooms—anything. We tell the kids, "Get on, spend an hour, then log off." Unfortunately, though, we found that a time limit meant nothing. Exposure to inappropriate language and sexual content can happen in seconds.

## Unplugging the Internet

We also have the computer placed in the den. We go in and out of that room all the time, so we figured that the kids would have some accountability. But again, things happen so fast. You can't be over their shoulder monitoring every conversation. Did you know there is a code for that? POS means "parent over shoulder." It's a warning to your chat buddies that someone is watching so they shouldn't say anything stupid.

### So you were really trying to safeguard the kids. What happened?

**Jim:** Even with the filtering done by our software, we still found some really sick stuff from these e-messenger conversations. We came across this stuff accidentally (though I don't disagree with checking deleted messages). I wonder sometimes if Kit almost wanted us to find it. The more we looked, the worse it became.

### Was this stuff from a friend of hers?

**Jim:** Well, yes and no. You see, when you are part of a chat room, you not only send and receive from your buddy list, you also connect with the other people in that chat room—most of whom are complete strangers. So, because the sender's screen name doesn't say who he actually is, he has total anonymity. It could be a fifteen-year-old or a fifty-five-year-old. We don't know.

### Do you think parents should check up on their children?

**Jim:** Absolutely. If a stranger came to your door and spent an hour and a half with your kid, wouldn't you listen in? Wouldn't you check up on the guy? We are a family that looks out for each other. Until the kids are adults, we have to protect them.

### You tried to safeguard the Internet use, but nothing worked for you. So what was your solution?

**Jim:** In our house, the solution was clear. No more Internet. We canceled the service.

### How did that go over with the kids?

**Jim:** They'll adjust. We had to be the parents; we had to make the tough decision. It was a sacrifice for Mollie and me, too, but the dangers are too great. The cons outweighed the convenience for us.

### Any advice for other parents?

**Jim:** Don't be afraid to take action. Be the parent. I see students every day who crave limits and no one says "no" to them. We know more than our kids; we can discern what they can't. They really need us to step in and protect them.

twelve

Train a child in the way he should go,
and when he is old he will not turn from it. (Proverbs 22:6)

A family we know installed an electric dog fence. They lived on a very busy street and felt that the invisible fence was the best way to protect their dog. Part of the installation was instruction for the family on how to train the dog to the new boundary. The two-year-old retriever had been accustomed to coming and going where and when he pleased, so you can imagine the rude awakening he had the first time he crossed the invisible fence. Zap! Painful for the dog and painful for the family that had to watch the first few "training experiences."

Sometimes we have invisible fences for our kids. We have boundaries, but no one knows about them until they've been zapped. Many of the families I surveyed found it difficult at first to identify rules or standards about dating and purity. Their first response was, "We don't really have any rules." OK, what happens when your fourteen-year-old daughter suddenly announces that she's going out with a twenty-year-old boy from a neighborhood across town? Here's another: It's 11:30 p.m. and your sixteen-year-old son takes his girlfriend (who looks like she's twenty-seven) up to his bedroom to watch MTV. I'll bet that all of a sudden you've got rules!

# Setting Reasonable Rules

The value of setting reasonable family rules and standards is inestimable. Without rules, children feel insecure and become confused about where the boundaries are. They are startled when you "zap" them with the invisible fence of sudden rules. Some standards may be spoken, some may be understood, but we must be sure our children know when they are close to hitting the fence. As one mom recently told me, "If they never *hear* the word 'no,' they won't know how to say it."

Did you ever see a cement truck pour wet cement? It oozes down a chute like pancake batter, then is shaped and smoothed by trowels and brushes. Within minutes it looks solid—ask any cat who has had a run-in with it. Those paw prints will be there forever. The values we teach our children are like impressions made on wet cement. But I'll warn you, there are cats in the neighborhood waiting to make their own impressions on your child's life. If you wait too long, the cement of your child's life will be set and it will be harder to repair. Communicating the family rules to your children at an early age can help you "pour" a foundation for future conversations. The sooner these principles are impressed upon your children, the better chance they will be "set" in a permanent way.

Healthy boundaries protect our kids rather than punish them. One of the most important areas around which boundaries must be set is dating. Josh McDowell's book *Why Wait?* reports a dramatic statistic that opened my eyes to the need for dating standards. Ninety-one percent of girls who begin dating at age twelve have sex before high school graduation. That number changes to fifty-six percent if dating begins at age thirteen and drops to only twenty percent when girls postpone dating until age sixteen. By creating this one boundary—the age dating begins—a parent increases his child's chance for success by seventy percent![1]

So, realizing that rules play a vital role in the future of our children, I asked our Reality Parenting contributors for some sample rules. I was surprised when they all quickly qualified their statements by saying that the rules *had* to be given in a context of ongoing love and support. The context, they felt, was in many ways a more important component than the rules themselves. So, I have distilled their conversations and thoughts into the seven guidelines listed below.

## The Guidelines

1. *Determine some rules for dating far in advance.* If a girl knows she won't be dating until age sixteen, she probably won't start bugging you about it at thirteen (but, she may begin *begging* at fifteen). If a boy knows he can't be alone in the house with his girlfriend, he'll have to make other plans or pay the consequences.
2. *Be reasonable.* Make sure your standards are attainable and be willing to talk about them without turning the discussion into a power struggle between you and your kids.
3. *Be sure of the definitions.* "When you're older" is vague and assumes that your children think of themselves as "younger." When you use the word *dating*, it may have a whole different meaning to a fifteen-year-old than it does to you. Keep in mind that phrases like "getting friendly," "hooking up" or "hanging out" probably have sexual implications. Know how your words will be translated by your teen. Make sure everyone's definitions are the same.

4. *Be in agreement with your spouse and/or other parents.* It is essential that you and your spouse communicate the family's guidelines in a unified way. Though total agreement is not always attainable, parents should support each other's values and standards whenever possible.

   A teenager can easily play a game of "nice parent/ mean parent" if you are not communicating a sense of agreement about the rules and the consequences. It is also extremely helpful to have agreement with former spouses, grandparents and stepparents so that the child encounters consistency on all fronts. Personal differences and past hurts must be put aside at this point for the benefit of your children. Conflict over the rules is more likely to cause rebellion than the rules themselves.

5. *Find things to say "yes" to.* Providing alternative social situations will stave off the date-to-be-popular instinct. Find appropriate, well-chaperoned social experiences for your kids. Open your home to be the place other kids will want to come. The "no dating until you are sixteen" rule may have a few exceptions, like a school dance, for instance. An 11:00 p.m. curfew may be extended from time to time for a special concert or group event. However, you need to make it clear that other than the specific exceptions you allow, the rules must be followed.

6. *Don't apologize for the rules.* Setting the rules is your job—you're the parent. Be confident and upbeat about them.

7. *Find others who share your family's rules.* You are not alone. Seeking out others who set high standards for their kids must be a priority. Bring up the subject any-

where you meet other parents—at work, at the gym, at the PTA or where you worship.

## Note:

1. Josh McDowell, *Why Wait? What You Need to Know About the Teen Sexuality Crisis* (Nashville, TN: Thomas Nelson, 1987), p. 79.

## Jane and Glen

Jane and Glen don't consider themselves strict parents. They have an easy-going parenting style and have set reasonable expectations for their two boys. Early in the boys' teen years, Jane and Glen established some ground rules about cars, phone calls and music choices, carefully picking their battles and giving the boys a blend of freedom and responsibility. One situation that defined the family standards came from what has become a growing trend among high schoolers: the coed sleepover.

**Jane:** Pete was going to take Brittanie to the homecoming dance. She's just a friend from the band, a real nice girl; all the kids in the band are nice kids. Anyway, plans were being made for what to wear and what corsage to buy. The kids were excited about the band playing at the game and then going to the dance. It was a really fun time for Pete. So when I asked him who was driving home, he told me that everyone was going to Brittanie's house after the dance for a sleepover. "Everyone" meaning the gang at school that they hang out with.

### When I hear "sleepover," I think of fourth grade girls' slumber parties. Do high schoolers have sleepovers?

**Jane:** This is very popular now—parents let their kids stay over after a dance or late-night event. The parties are supposed to be chaperoned, but get real—who is going to stay up all night long to keep an eye on Ken and Barbie? I don't think it's a wise choice for a six-foot, hormone-packed teenager to spend the night snuggling next to his date. We want the kids to control themselves and then

# The Sleepover

we throw them into a nearly impossible situation? So, Glen and I said "no" to the sleepover.

## How did that go with Pete?

**Jane:** His first question was, "Why? Don't you trust me?" Then came the arguments: His friends were all good kids, nothing was going to happen, Brittanie is not his type anyway . . . she's just a friend. The answer was still "no." Then came, "But *everyone* will be there but me. Everyone's parents are OK with this. What is *wrong* with you?"

That was the part that bugged me the most. Everyone else's parents said "yes." "Nothing is wrong with us," I told him. "I want to know what's wrong with all of them!"

## Is it frustrating to be the only parent saying "no"?

**Jane:** I remember my parents saying as they were about to punish me, "This is going to hurt me more than it is you." And I remember thinking to myself, *I doubt it*. But at the time when Pete was questioning my sanity, I really found it hard to do what I thought was right. It hurt me to watch Pete miss out on a party with his friends. Just like watching a baby receive a shot, you know it is necessary, but it kills you to go through with it.

## Are you saying that you don't trust Pete?

**Jane:** Pete's a great kid and he has a super group of friends. But they're kids. They lie around on each other and snuggle all cozy in front of the TV. It's a hormonal time bomb. No one is so strong that they can handle *any* temptation. I trust my husband, but I wouldn't want him to share a hotel room with a female coworker. I'm trustworthy, but please don't put a box of chocolates in front of me when I'm on a diet. We're really not being fair to these kids. In the Lord's Prayer, Jesus urges us to pray, "Lead us not into temptation" (Matthew 6:13). So why do we lead our teenagers there?

At midnight, I went over to the party and picked up my seventeen-year-old son. He was the only one to leave the party early. It was a real sight. There he was, a six-foot-three-inch, 200-pound kid going home with his mommy. I was really beginning to second-guess myself. Was I the *only* parent who thought this was a bad idea?

## So, Pete, how did you feel about the whole thing?

**Pete:** I didn't talk to my mom the whole way home after she picked me up at the party. Or the whole next day, either. It was weird, though, because even though I was embarrassed and mad, I knew inside that she was right. It's just so geeky to do the right thing sometimes.

## Does purity make you a geek?

**Pete:** I'll never be the most popular kid at school, if that's what you mean. But I have some friends who think like I do. You just decide who your friends are going to be, and then you stick with them. Later on I found out that the party pretty much went nowhere after I left. Those guys are all still my friends, so what did I miss, really?

## Jane, do you have any advice for parents out there?

**Jane:** Don't let other parenting styles get you down. You're going to get pressure that every other parent is allowing this or that to go on. I know of parents who provide alcohol at their kids' parties. Some drop their kids off at the cinema to see whatever R-rated movie is playing. Parents have peer pressure too—we feel geeky and out of step sometimes too. No matter what other families allow, you *must* do the right thing. And, yes, it is tough for your kids, but they're going to live. They may even grow up to thank us. Right, Pete? Pete?

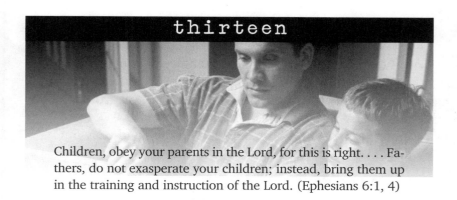

## thirteen

Children, obey your parents in the Lord, for this is right. . . . Fathers, do not exasperate your children; instead, bring them up in the training and instruction of the Lord. (Ephesians 6:1, 4)

When reviewing and considering the rules that follow, remember that they are a sampling of what some families found to be effective, fair and loving. I hope their ideas become a springboard for setting your own family standards.

## Rules from Reality Parents

### Charles and Rita:

We have set a curfew. In middle school, the kids had to be home by ten o'clock at night. High school curfew was ten o'clock on weeknights, eleven on the weekends. If the curfew was broken, a privilege (using the car, allowance, etc.) was removed. We enforced the curfew and only made exceptions when they were discussed ahead of time.

### Jane and Glen:

Until our kids were driving themselves, we did not allow them to ride in other people's cars without an adult driver. This was a

# Realistic Rules

difficult rule to keep and meant that we had to do a lot of carpooling, but there had been so many teens involved in car accidents in our district that we felt it was worth the sacrifice. We also double-dated with our kids. We would treat them to a nice dinner with their date and we would drive. We really learned a lot from those dates.

## Linda and Ron:

We asked our son to always walk up to the door and ask to meet the parents of the girl he was taking out. We expected the same from young men who took out our daughter. We feel that it is a sign of respect and maturity. Likewise, we asked our daughter to find out as much as she could about her date's family ahead of time. All plans for social activities had to be cleared with us first. Everyone's schedule is so crazy that we had to make this a rule.

## Charles and Rita:

We limited the number of "dates" our daughter could go on during the week. When she began dating, she was out with the same boy five nights in a row. We knew this was moving along too quickly and asked her to limit her dates with that boy to two nights per week only. This gave her a lot more breathing room and kept her in touch with her friends and activities.

## Jane and Glen:

Our kids are not allowed to be in a house alone with their girlfriends. "No exceptions" means that there must be more communication about schedules. The kids need to know when we'll be home if they want to hang out there. Having a cell phone really helps with this. Likewise, our sons must discuss this rule with their girlfriends' parents. This has improved respect and communication in the girls' homes as well.

## Mario and Gina:

In our house, the kids aren't allowed to date until they reach sixteen. This really frees them up because they're under no pressure to pursue a relationship. We have found that they go into situations with a different mind-set than other kids. They don't have to scheme, plan, sneak or manipulate others to get alone with a girl or guy.

We had several discussions about what a date really is and determined that any social outing where one boy was paired up with one girl would be considered a date. Once the rule was set, we thought of several exceptions we would be willing to make. One was church dances. The other was the homecoming dance at school. Another way we made this rule work was to make our home an enjoyable place to be. We wanted other kids to feel comfortable dropping in any time. Our kids had a social life here at home.

## Jim and Mollie:

The phone became a problem for our daughter. Knowing she was not allowed to "date," Kit began to use the phone to call boys she liked. So, we made a few phone rules: No calling anyone after 9 o'clock.; no calling boys unless for a specific purpose. We also put a time limit on calls.

## Todd and Callie:

Becky has a cell phone. She buys a prepaid number of minutes with her allowance. When the minutes are gone, she's done until she can afford to pay for more. This has helped her budget her time on the phone.

## Jim and Mollie:

We won't drop our kids off at the mall. We got the most criticism about this rule. Parents were just dropping off their fourteen- and fifteen-year-old kids at the mall to hang out. "Malling" has led many teens we know to try shoplifting, cigarettes, drugs and even sex (they go out to someone's car in the parking lot).

## Linda and Ron:

We had to make some rules about clothing and appearance. It seemed like most girls Keisha's age were getting away with wearing next to nothing. If you are practically naked in front of people you hardly know, what are you saving for marriage? Of course we got into arguments about it—it's difficult for young girls to understand the message they send. They just think they look cute; they don't realize how men's minds work. We asked our kids to come up with some reasonable boundaries about clothes, but we had final veto power on buying or wearing outfits that were too revealing.

## Jane and Glen:

No parties with girls and guys together until age sixteen and no coed sleepovers. Exceptions are sports receptions, cast parties and other large, well-chaperoned events. We found that parties put a lot of pressure on kids to "pair up" just to fit in.

- Write down the first three dating rules that pop into your mind.

- Are they reasonable, definable and attainable?
- Find time to talk through your ideas with your spouse (or others who share parenting) this week.
- When you have determined the basic guidelines, write them out.
- Consider ways to confidently share those family rules with your kids. Think about when and how you will share them.

## Todd and Callie

Divorce is a reality for over one-third of America's teenagers.[1] Even under the most congenial circumstances, the divorced couple may find themselves at odds over parenting styles. As a result, two sets of rules emerge—one for Mom's house and one for Dad's. When a child is growing up in both homes, confusion and conflict can intensify through the teen years.

Todd and Callie have four children. Each brought one child into the marriage, then they had two more of their own, making a truly blended family. Todd's oldest daughter, Becky, is thirteen and lives with her mother in a town forty minutes away from Todd's home. She visits Todd and Callie's house every other weekend.

**Todd:** The biggest obstacle for me is the two sets of rules. At her mom's house, Becky is allowed to have a boyfriend and a cell phone and to see any movies she wants. Because her mom works, Becky is home alone after school with no supervision. And now that she's a teenager, she pushes all the limits. At my house, it's a different story. There is a curfew, TV limits, chores to do and limited phone privileges. We clash over it; she thinks my rules are stupid. But I'm her dad and I'm really concerned. There are potential battles on many fronts. For one thing, my wife, Callie, handles things differently than I would sometimes. But I back her up, and we try to make a unified stand. Also, my ex-wife and I often disagree on Becky's upbringing. Don't even get me started on Becky's stepdad.

## Two Homes, Two Sets of Rules

## *Wow, she's got a boyfriend? What does "boy-friend" mean to a thirteen-year-old?*

**Todd:** Good question. I guess it means that they have an exclusive relationship. I call it a "childlike commitment." They see movies together and go to school dances every other weekend. Wesley is a nice kid and is in the same grade at school. They met playing soccer. His mom is very strict—she keeps her eyes open. But they are too young to be dating. How long can an innocent romance go on before things begin to happen? And if she's experiencing these things at thirteen, what will she be doing at fifteen or sixteen? I know that the earlier dating begins, the more likely sex will begin early too.

## *So what strategies have worked for you?*

**Todd:** My wife, Callie, bless her heart, goes to see some of the movies Becky and Wesley see together. She wants to find out what Becky is being influenced by. This helps us to know what we're up against.

I try to build my relationship with Becky so that she's not looking for love in the wrong place. We go on dates. I take her out, one-on-one. And that's where we communicate about the rules and then share our feelings when our tempers are cool. But I have to guard that time. As her social life increases, a million things arise that could push our plans off the calendar. But I make sure we keep the date.

## *What about Becky's mom? How do you handle the conflicts over the rules?*

**Todd:** I don't want to set this up as bad parent versus good parent. My ex-wife has done a good job with many issues like grades, clothes and other things. However, we don't see eye-to-eye on the subject of dating. What we do have in common, however, is our love for Becky and so we have an appointment once in a while to review the situation and hear each other's concerns.

## So you have a face-to-face meeting?

**Todd:** Yes, once every other month, we have an appointment to meet at a neutral place. We go over the key issues and conflicts—most everything we discuss has to do with Becky. Sometimes we disagree and it doesn't seem productive, but it keeps communication lines open. We keep it cool and businesslike.

## Do you have any advice for other parents in the same boat?

**Todd:** Love your kids. Love them enough to be tough with them on things. I have to hold to my standards no matter what Becky's mom does. I'm clear about the rules for my home, and I hope that my concern for Becky is translated in a way that she knows she's loved and cared for.

If it were in my power, I would not allow Becky to date until she was sixteen or seventeen years old. So many issues could be avoided with that one rule. It takes a great deal of energy to work things out between the two families because, like I said, you have so many more people involved. But Becky is my daughter, and she's worth it.

# Note:

1. Statistics and other information on divorce available on-line from: <http://www.divorcereform.org>.

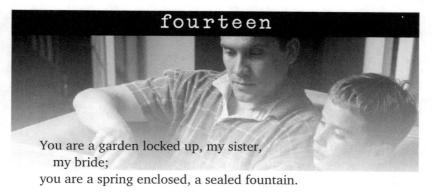

## fourteen

You are a garden locked up, my sister,
   my bride;
you are a spring enclosed, a sealed fountain.

(Song of Solomon 4:12)

What shall we do for our sister
   for the day she is spoken for?
If she is a wall,
   we will build towers of silver on her.
If she is a door,
   we will enclose her with panels of cedar.

(Song of Solomon 8:8-9)

These verses from Song of Solomon give us two wonderful word pictures. The first is a protected place, a sealed fountain inside of a locked garden. This is clearly the picture of virginity. Imagine a beautiful garden blazing with color, heavy with fruit and alive with a wonderful aroma that wafts over its walls. The garden and its source of water are sealed off. No casual tourist may enter, only one who would tend the garden and enjoy its fruits exclusively. But who planted the garden, and who built the wall? Who locked its gates?

## Giving Our B.E.S.T.

As parents, we are our children's caretakers. By building relationships and setting reasonable rules, we protect our teenagers' gardens.

The second illustration is the contrast between a wall and a door. Some kids will be strong in the face of sexual temptation. They will stand like a wall. We are encouraged to decorate that wall with towers of silver. Praising your strong child is like decorating his wall. Reward him and tell others how proud you are of his strength and character. Just like putting his trophies on a shelf or hanging blue ribbons on a wall, "decorate" your child. Make him a wall of fame.

Other children might be more like a door. They open up to exploration and risk. When your child opens the door by seeking sexual attention and affection, strangers may enter the garden to use its great fruits. This is a child who needs to be enclosed with panels of cedar. Cedar is delicious-smelling wood used for decorative and aromatic purposes. It is durable and strong. Loving boundaries and limits are like sweet-smelling panels that enclose and protect. Without them, the doors will swing open.

Is your child a door or a wall? How will you protect the garden growing inside his heart? What are some practical ways to help our kids face the dating years? Remember to give them the B.E.S.T.:

# **Build Boundaries**

Help your child determine the best boundaries for the dating years. I ask students to make a list of three things they will never do and three places they will never go. Kids come up with some thoughtful ideas: Never get in a car with someone you don't know, never go to a party when there aren't adults around, etc. I also encourage teens to know their "geography." There are several questions that can help kids keep good "geography": "Where am I?"; "What time is it?"; "Who's in control?"; "What is the plan?" These sound like questions a parent should be asking,  but it is important that your kids begin to ask these questions of themselves. Liberty isn't doing what you please; it is the freedom to do what is right. Likewise, to be mature means to be free to have fun in a responsible manner.

Creative date ideas like the ones mentioned earlier in this book are part of building boundaries. Making a list of date ideas from A to Z is a fun exercise. (Go to an Air show, go Bike riding, make Cookies, feed the Ducks . . . get the idea?) Each idea should be with a group, during the day and not expensive. Group dating is a safer way for children to meet and get to know the opposite sex. Make sure your child knows at least two other people in the group. Dates that are during the daylight hours and that are cheap help keep the pressure off too.

Challenge your teens to show affection without touch. Many kids seem to rely on physical touch to demonstrate love and affection. This is perfectly appropriate with family members, but not when the touch is sexual. Ask them if they could communicate care and kindness for a girlfriend or boyfriend without holding hands, lying all over each other and sexual touch. See what they come up with. (One word of caution here. Many boys consider saying "I love you" to be an answer to this challenge. These three words are the most powerful words a boy could ever say to a young lady. If he truly means it, his next words should be, "Would you marry me?")

## Establish Emergency Exits

Next time you stay at a motel, close the door and show your kids the escape route. Point out that the escape route is there for emergencies. Also point out that life is full of emergencies. When teens begin to go out together, there is often no plan, no goal, just the adventure of going out to see what happens. Though this sounds carefree and spontaneous, it usually produces a boring evening of driving around with nothing to do. If something eventful does happen, kids may find they need an escape plan. Alcohol, drugs, speeding and sex aren't things that "just happen" to kids. The little decisions that they make (or don't make) can lead to trouble. We need to help them avoid the dangers by planning for an unexpected emergency.

Most date rape occurs because kids don't have an escape route. A ride home, a cell phone or a strong group of friends all provide ways of escape from potentially harmful situations. Consider having phone code. Families agree on a coded message that means, "I'm uncomfortable in this situation, and I need a way out without embarrassing myself." When a situation seems out of control, a teen may say, "Oh, no, it's ten o'clock. I'm supposed to check in with my mom." The coded check-in phone call might be, "What? I have to come home now?! Well, OK, let me tell you where I am." The parent gets the picture: My child is in trouble; I'm on my way. This strategy takes all the pressure off the child and places it on the parents. When friends ask why the sudden change in plans, the teen can simply blame it on his lame parents. (That's you!)

## Set Standards

"If you don't set standards for yourself, someone else will set them for you." I've said this to thousands of teenagers.

Setting your sights high tells the world how you feel about yourself. Like Keisha said earlier in the book, "I'm above all that." Help to refine your child's choices about life and love. Ask the child to make a list of qualities he or she is looking for in a boy or girl. Help the child think about how he wants to be treated and the kind of reputation he wants to have. Encourage him to set high standards for how he dresses and talks. You should talk to him about other things that influence his standards. Ask him questions like: How do movies and other media measure up to those standards? How do your friends measure up to those standards? Your child is precious and has a unique destiny. The higher he aims now, the closer he will be to the target.

## Take Your Time

Postpone dating as long as possible. I know that this may be difficult in some homes, but the age at which dating begins is the single most influential factor in predicting sexual debut, teen pregnancy, STD infection and many forms of depression. Adolescents should be free from those worries. God's plan for sex was to provide a lifelong marriage and to protect us from the ravages of heartbreak and disease. As the wisdom of His plan unfolds over the teen years, fill the place in your child's heart that longs for acceptance, intimacy and unconditional love. Your child's first and best asset is you. So take your time, encourage your child's heart, enjoy the process of building the parent/child relationship. The investment will last a lifetime.

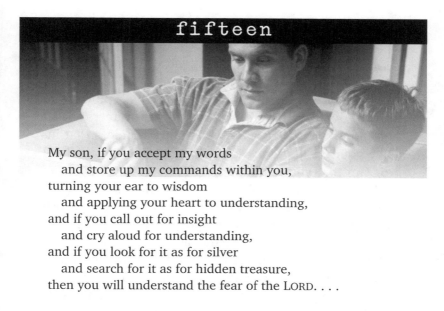

## fifteen

My son, if you accept my words
    and store up my commands within you,
turning your ear to wisdom
    and applying your heart to understanding,
and if you call out for insight
    and cry aloud for understanding,
and if you look for it as for silver
    and search for it as for hidden treasure,
then you will understand the fear of the LORD. . . .

He is a shield to those whose walk is blameless,
    for he guards the course of the just
and protects the way of his faithful ones.

(Proverbs 2:1-5, 7-8)

## Question One:

*My sixth-grader's health class is showing a video on reproduction and I have to sign the permission slip that allows my child to view the video. I'm not sure what the content is and I'm not comfortable with having my child exposed to something with potentially questionable material. But, if I don't sign the slip, I'm afraid my child will feel embarrassed. What should I do?*

This is a very common dilemma. We're just cruising along through the school year when suddenly "the note" appears. It's a

## Tough Questions

permission slip for sex education and it's usually due the very next day. What do you do?

When you develop a vision for your child's purity, you want to do everything in your power to protect that vision. Sometimes that will mean making choices that involve your child's education. When it comes to a school program that you know nothing about, I say, "When in doubt, pull them out." You will not be the first or the last parent to keep a child out of a class on sex. The absence will probably go unnoticed if you make arrangements with the teacher to keep the dismissal discreet.

You should view the arrival of that permission slip as the trigger to begin teaching your child your family's vision regarding sexuality and purity. But we can do more than just opt out of sex education. The following three steps not only help to preserve your child's innocence, but will give other families a glimpse of your vision as well.

First, *establish a relationship* with your school. Visit staff and teachers often, preferably with cookies or some other sort of treat. Working parents can send notes of encouragement, help with fund-raising and volunteer for special projects. Be the parent who catches the school doing something right. You don't have to be on the school board to make a positive impact. By establishing a rapport with the school staff and teachers, you'll earn the right to be heard if and when a conflict arises.

Second, *examine the curriculum*. Long before "the note" comes home, ask if you can view the videos and look over the resources and text for sex education. Some schools offer a parent review time. If your school doesn't, schedule a time early in the fall on your own and suggest that the school might want to consider setting up a parent review time in the future. If you have elementary-age children, start asking questions of the school when they are in third or fourth grade. Be positive, but critical. As you examine the products, ask the following questions:

- Is the content age-appropriate? Your gut feeling on this is usually right. Generally fourth- and fifth-grade programs will discuss physical changes that occur in adolescence. The male/female reproductive systems are usually introduced in seventh and eighth grades. High school programs give more detail on disease, pregnancy and—hopefully—strategies for saying "no" to premarital sex. It is appropriate to introduce marriage as the basis for building a family at any age. Privacy, modesty, rejecting unwanted touch and affection are also themes that will benefit any age group.

- Is the material current? Videos and texts for older teens have a short shelf life. STD information changes dramatically every three years or so, so videos and other information need to be updated at least that frequently. I actually recently previewed a video at a local senior high school that showed a birth control method that had been off the market for almost fifteen years! There are some obvious things that can tip you off that a video is out of date. Hairstyles are a dead giveaway for the production date. Texts should have a copyright or revision date, so be sure to look for it. Also look at any posters, articles and resources the individual teacher may have added to the program to make sure they are up-to-date and appropriate.

- Do they separate boys from girls? Gender-separate sex education respects a natural sense of modesty. If a student has questions, he is more likely to ask in a gender-separate classroom. Also, material can be presented in a more mature manner and teasing is less likely to be a problem. Most schools continue to provide gender-separate classes at the elementary level. Yours should too. It is inconvenient for schools to provide two classrooms and two teachers for separate gender classes, but not impossible. If your child's school does not employ this approach, offer suggestions about how to make it work.

- Does it portray marriage in a positive way? Look for the word "marriage" rather than "long-term committed relationship." Listen for "spouse," "husband" or "wife" instead of "partner."

- Does it stay on track? Discussions promoting homosexuality, sexual play and outercourse are common in today's classrooms. So are demonstrations like putting condoms on bananas. These so-called "comprehensive" approaches send a mixed message and shift the focus away from abstinence. Check to see if all parts of the program work together to promote abstinence until marriage.

Third, *entertain alternatives*. Many times a school uses what it has on the shelf. Look for practical ways to help the staff find alternatives. Ask for catalogues of sex-ed products that offer trial viewing. Research assembly speakers and offer to raise money to pay their fees. High quality, affordable resources that promote purity and sexual health *are* available. If your school won't commit to using them, find a

church or civic group that will and put on a program outside the school.

## Question Two:

*I know that my daughter is sexually active. Wouldn't it be
better for her to go on the pill rather than getting herself
into more trouble?*

Let's answer that question by looking at two miscon-
ceptions about sex. First, it is a common notion that pregnancy is the worst thing that could happen to our teenage
daughters. This is partly because pregnancy is so public.
It is tough to hide. There will be shame and embarrassment for the whole family. Teen pregnancy also leads to a
tough choice between single parenting, early marriage,
adoption or abortion.

Each of these options will forever change a teenager's
life. Single parenting means putting future goals aside for
a time. It is also a near-guarantee of increased financial
hardship. Early marriage can be a solution only for couples willing to commit to ongoing accountability. But any
parent knows this is a tough way to begin a marriage.
Adoption is one of the most courageous choices. It gives
life and then releases the baby to be raised by a family
longing for a child of their own. But for a young birth
mother, adoption is not an easy choice and requires expert counseling and support. Abortion takes the life of a
child. It may seem like a quick fix but it can leave a scar
from which many women will never find healing.

Embarrassed, angry, their dreams for their teenager
shattered, many parents feel that a positive pregnancy
test means that their daughter's life is over. In the face of
these potential hardships, providing your teenage daugh-

ter with a method of birth control may look like the answer—a safety precaution "just in case."

However, sexual activity invites a range of other consequences into your child's life that can have just as great an impact as pregnancy. Sexually transmitted diseases (STDs), guilt, regret, low self-esteem, poor relationships and depression are all serious outcomes of sexual intimacy outside of marriage. Most birth control methods reduce the risk of only one of those consequences—pregnancy. They will not protect the heart or the mind and many will provide no protection whatsoever against sexually transmitted diseases. Even the condom has a high failure rate for preventing the transmission of viral STDs.[1] By encouraging your son or daughter to avoid only the problem of pregnancy, you send a message that the emotional and relational part of sex is not important. You also convey the idea that procreation can be completely removed from the sex act. Many chemical birth control methods carry great risks of side effects, and some make the body even more susceptible to disease. Also, none are 100 percent effective, so the possibility of pregnancy always exists.

The second common misconception about sex is the assumption that once a teen has begun having sex, he can't return to a pure lifestyle. Once, while I was counseling a young teenage girl to consider signing a pledge card to say "no" to sex, her mother interrupted and said, "What? She can't say 'no.' Once you start, you can't stop." I don't know whether it was repentance or defiance, but that fifteen-year-old gave her mother quite a look and then signed a Chastity Challenge purity pledge card. She kept her pledge.

If your child is sexually active, he has chosen to go down a certain road. But that child is never so far gone that he cannot return to secondary virginity. It is your love and acceptance that is needed more than anything at such a time. Just think: In the time it would take to educate your child about birth control, have him or her get a physical examination and have a form of birth control prescribed, you could take major steps in offering restoration and healing and in the renewal of your relationship. Don't settle for a second-best approach.

## Question Three:

*My ex-husband lives with his girlfriend, and my kids visit him every other weekend and on some holidays. I don't approve of the situation, but the kids like his girlfriend and I don't want to be negative toward their dad. What should I say about it?*

You are wise to encourage your children to respect their father and his girlfriend. At the same time, you can still continue to build a vision of a happy, healthy marriage in your child's life. It is a tough balance to love a person while you disagree with his behavior. Your response can be loving and compassionate while continuing to build on the foundation of the truth of God's Word.

According to the U.S. Census, cohabitation, or "living together," has increased eight-fold since 1970. Four million heterosexual couples are cohabiting in America today. Research suggests that couples who choose to live together rather than marry are disillusioned with marriage. Many have been married previously; many more have grown up in homes broken by divorce. On the surface, cohabitation sounds like a test drive, a trial to see if a future marriage will work out. Fear of a future breakup along with a desire for intimacy makes living together without long-term commitment appealing to many people.

However, in sharp contradiction to the assumptions many people make about cohabitation, the National Opinion Research Center at the University of Chicago has found that cohabitation leads to short-term relationships and few commitments to marriage.[2] Couples who live together make less money and are more likely to physically abuse one another than married couples.[3] A study from Penn State University finds that couples who live together before marriage have poorer communication skills and a higher likelihood of separation and divorce.[4] In all of my rather extensive research on this subject, I have come across absolutely no evidence to show that living together before marriage benefits couples.

Marriage, on the other hand, is getting rave reviews. In their book *The Case for Marriage*, Linda J. Waite and Maggie Gallagher give compelling reasons to promote marriage to our children. Some of these reasons are: Married people live longer, are wealthier, have more fulfilling sex and have it more often than their unmarried counterparts. Children raised in homes with an intact marriage do better in school and are less likely to use drugs.[5]

## Question Four:

*My son is fifteen and feels like he is the only virgin in his school. We're proud of him for taking a stand, but we know he is excluded from parties and social events because of his strong morals. We're also afraid that his resolve will weaken because of the teasing he gets. How can we encourage him?*

It is heartbreaking to watch our kids go through trials. Even when we know that our children are doing the right thing, we want to spare them the pain of isolation and from being ridiculed by their peers. In a world where sex seems to bring popularity and respect, teens perceive that kids who are "fast" or "easy" will be invited to all the parties and have all the fun.

Once again, we want to start by arming our children with the truth. Let us address the fallacy that "everyone is doing it." Fifty-one percent of graduating high school seniors report that they have never had sex.[6] That puts virgins in the majority for the first time in fifteen years, a fact which means that most likely more than half of your son's class would be in this category. The difficult part, however, is convincing him of this fact. One way would be to encourage him to get involved in a program that works to build positive peer pressure in school communities. These types of programs have had a great impact, bringing school communities to a point where virginity is the norm and sex is considered off-limits.

These programs include The Silver Ring Thing and True Love Waits. The Silver Ring Thing communicates the abstinence message in such an inviting way that teens jump at the chance to wear the silver ring which becomes the symbol of their commitment. After less than two years of saturating local high schools, the silver ring has become "cool."

True Love Waits is a national program with built-in support. True Love Waits programs conclude with a pledge ceremony in which students sign a card indicating their commitment to wait for sex until marriage. Over 1 million teens have signed this pledge.

So, when your son gets a bad case of the "everyone's doing it but me" blues, point him to the True Love Waits Web site (http://www.lifeway.com/tlw/) or The Silver Ring

Thing Web site (http://www.silverringthing.com). By checking out these Web sites and getting involved with either of these programs, he will be put in touch with a larger world and receive the affirmation that there are thousands of people out there who used to feel the same way.

## Question Five:

*Our son has recently told us that several of the guys in his class have been questioning his manhood because he has taken a strong stance against premarital sex. What should we tell him?*

Many teens, especially boys, are plagued with questions like, "Does waiting for sex indicate that your sex drives aren't as strong as they should be?" or "Is a virgin repressing something or perhaps hiding homosexual tendencies?" Encourage your teenage son by telling him that a man's strength and power are exhibited not when he acts on his urges but when he controls and bridles those urges. It takes great strength to say "no" when everything in you says "yes." In his book *Raising a Modern-Day Knight*, Dr. Robert Lewis encourages fathers to pass along the principles of manhood. "Leadership," says Lewis, "demands that men have the courage to master their passions and bridle themselves with the principle of truth. . . . The courage to *lead with truth* rather than surrender to feelings always separates the men from the boys."[7]

Leadership is developed through the testing of our values. Integrity is doing the right thing when no one is looking. An example of leadership and integrity in the face of sexual temptation is found in Genesis 39, the story of Joseph. You may remember Joseph as the boy with the strange dreams and the coat of many colors. This happy dreamer was lured into a pit by his brothers and left for dead. They took his blood-stained coat home to prove to their father that Joseph was dead. But a group of slave traders passed the pit and took Joseph to Egypt, where he was sold as a slave.

By age seventeen, Joseph was a handsome, hardworking slave in the house of Potiphar, a wealthy and influential leader in Egypt. Potiphar's wife noticed this good-looking young guy and tried to seduce him. Every day, the Bible says, she asked him to have sex with her. Now remember, Joseph was in his prime, and this woman was wealthy, beautiful and used to getting anything she wanted. Many men would have given in. But Joseph resisted. One day, Mrs. Potiphar sent everyone home early. Her husband was away and she thought that it was the perfect chance to have Joseph all to herself. But, even when no one was looking, Joseph resisted. Was he gay? No, he was strong. And how was he rewarded for his faithfulness and virtue? Mrs. Potiphar accused Joseph of rape and he was sent to prison. Prison! For doing the right thing?

Waiting for sex can feel like dating prison for teens. It may seem dark, lonely and full of rats, but within the walls of this prison, God develops leadership and vision. When Joseph emerged from prison, he was positioned to save his generation from famine, starvation and death. Our children too can rise from "prison" to save their generation from heartbreak, disease and brokenness. Be patient as you encourage them through this time of obedience. The rewards are eternal.

## Question Six:

*I've heard a lot about lesbianism lately and how it has become chic for girls to "switch" from boys to girls. I'm afraid that my children are going to be exposed to this behavior in school, so I want to talk to them about it. What's the best way to do this?*

As parents, many of us feel panicked at the slightest mention of homosexuality. We may fear that bringing up the topic of homosexuality with our kids will plant ideas in their heads. We may also lack confidence about how to talk about such an explosive and sensitive issue. We may even want to bury our heads in the sand and never address the subject at all. However, an increasingly aggressive gay community has made this issue impossible to ignore.

Homosexuality is being marketed as an acceptable alternative lifestyle, a normal personality trait that one in ten people are born with. It seems like every new TV sitcom includes a clever, witty and articulate gay person. Celebrities become role models to young children and then come out of the closet on national news. Same-sex experimentation has become more and more common in America's middle schools and high schools, and we must prepare our kids to live in a culture where homosexuality is growing in acceptance.

However, we must first prepare *ourselves* to answer the questions and to give our children clear and understandable information regarding the biblical stance on homosexuality. A Christian who believes that God's Word sets the standard for sexual behavior will find that the Bible strongly prohibits homosexuality. First Corinthians 6:9-10 tells us that the sexually immoral, including those who practice homosexuality, "will not inherit the kingdom of God." Romans 1:21-32 explains the nature of sin and that homosexuality is one of a list of offenses that God detests. Homosexuality rejects God's magnificent design for mankind, which is the natural procreative wonder of intimacy between a husband and wife.

While these verses warn about the destructive nature of sin, they also remind us that we serve a compassionate God who desires that all men know Him and the power of His resurrection. Authors Stephen Arterburn and Jim Burns encourage Christians to separate the homosexual person from the act of homosexuality and consider them as two separate issues.

> Homosexuality is an inclination or desire for some-one of the same sex to provide emotional intimacy, acceptance, and/or affection. It describes the heart— the identity—of a person who isn't attracted to people of the opposite sex. It doesn't always result in homosexual behavior.
>
> Homosexual behavior, on the other hand, is the manifestation of that inclination and desire. The difference is significant. Lust is a sin, but inclination toward lust is not. The inclination toward homosexuality is not a sin, but the behavior, as outlined in Scripture, is.[8]

Just as we realize that we are all sinners and fall short of the glory of God, we need to realize that we should not condemn another person for his sin, but we must take a strong stand against his immoral behavior. The Bible is clear on the issue of homosexuality, just as it is on premarital sex, gossip, stealing and lying. It is also clear that God desires us to be holy and these are actions that "miss the mark" of God's holy standard for our lives.

As we are carefully and prayerfully preparing ourselves to discuss the issue of homosexuality with our children, we must consider the contexts in which our children may encounter it. We must also consider the possibility that one of our own children may display a tendency toward homosexuality.

For teens facing the issue of homosexuality today, I believe that we can separate same-sex relationships into two categories. First are those who engage in sex play with the same sex as a form of experimentation. They are driven by curiosity and encouraged by a culture that rewards wild, shocking sexual exploration. It is considered chic, trendy and cool. This behavior seems most prevalent in girls. With so many female celebrities confessing their openness to both sexes, the impression is given that young women can simply "switch" back and forth. Boys are portrayed as interested and fascinated by lesbian behavior, and girls think that boys will be more turned on by a girl who would do anything with anyone.

Parents are often blind to this behavior. Their child doesn't look or act gay. She seems to have normal relationships and is very popular. Kids too will deny the gay label. Even when caught in the act, girls will often claim they were only pretending or playing a joke, trying to "shock" someone they know. It will be extremely difficult to know whether they are masking sexual orientation confusion or just playing the role of a "party animal." Technically these girls are virgins, and they will act offended when confronted about sexual abstinence.

When you talk to your daughters and sons about same-sex affection, make sure they understand that purity is purity, no matter which sex we are talking about. Sexual play outside of marriage is prohibited by God. It cheapens physical intimacy. Sex is not a game, and all sexual affection should be cherished and meaningful. Teens willing to take these kinds of risks sexually will be prone to experimentation of all sorts. They will face identity confusion and labeling. While they may feel cool, crazy and popular in middle school, their high school experience will be increasingly empty and isolated.

The second category is made up of those engaged in a deep inner struggle with their sexual identity. In the same school where a girl may be celebrated for her willingness to "switch," a boy may be mercilessly teased and abused for behavior that resembles that of a "queer," or homosexual. Pay close attention to this teasing, for it can make a lifetime impact on your child.

The reasons for the sexual identity confusion that some kids experience may be difficult to pinpoint. Many homosexual adults find they share similar experiences, such as rejection, teasing, abuse and molestation, that may have contributed to their choice to be homosexual. We must do our best as parents to guard against these influences.

When discussing this issue, remind your kids that homosexuality is a poor second to pure sexuality. It is not how God designed our bodies to work and does not allow for building family and community. Homosexuals are people struggling with sin, just as we all do, so the people living that life should not be condemned, but the sin they are committing should be. To allow sin to go unrestrained is unloving and will not work for the ultimate good. If your child appears to be struggling, accept and love him or her, pray for wisdom with each word and action and seek expert help from a pastor or counselor who has demonstrated an ability to help others through a solid, biblical approach to the subject.

# Notes:

1. H. Bauer, et.al., "Genital Human Papilloma Virus Infection in Female University Students by a PRC-Based Method," *Journal of the American Medical Association*, 265:4, January 1991.

2. David Popenoe and Barbara Dafoe Whitehead, "Should We Live Together?: What Young Adults Need to Know about Cohabitation before Marriage," The National Marriage Project: The Next Generation Series. Available on-line from: <http://www.smartmarriages.com/cohabit.html>.

3. Willard F. Jabusch, "The Myth of Cohabitation: Cohabiting Couples Lack Both Specialization and Commitment in Their Relationships" [on-line], October 7, 2000. May 8, 2003. Available from: <http://www.findarticles.com/cf_0/PI/search.jhtml?magR=all+magazines&key=The+Myth+of+Cohabitation>.

4. William G. Axinn and Jennifer S. Barber, "Living Arrangements and Family Formation Attitudes in Early Adulthood," *Journal of Marriage and the Family*, 59: 1997, pp. 595-611.

5. Linda J. Waite and Maggie Gallagher, *The Case for Marriage: Why Married People Are Happier, Healthier and Better Off Financially* (New York: Doubleday, 2000), pp. 69-70.

6. "Youth Risk Behavior Surveillance" [on-line], *Morbidity and Mortality Weekly Report*, CPC, Vol. 49, No. SS-05, June 9, 2000. October 10, 2002. Available from: <http://www.cdc.gov/mmwr/preview/mmwrhtml/ss4905a1.htm>.

7. Robert Lewis, *Raising a Modern-Day Knight* (Colorado Springs, CO: Focus on the Family Publishers, 1999), pp. 56-7.

8. Stephen Arterburn and Jim Burns, *The Top Ten Dangers Teens Face* (Carol Stream, IL: Tyndale House Publishers, 1995), p. 179.

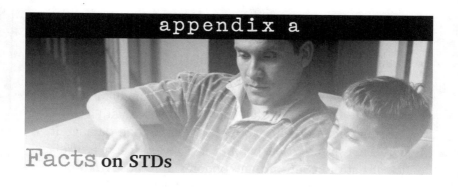

# Facts on STDs

oday there are over twenty-five sexually transmitted diseases, which cause 15.3 million infections per year. That's 30,000 new cases each day, making STDs the most reported infection in the United States. All twenty-five STDs cause damage to the body, and some STDs are life-threatening. Sexually active teens open themselves up to the tremendous risk of acquiring one of these STDs.[1] Let's take a closer look at a few of the most prevalent diseases.

Chlamydia, with three million cases each year, is the most common STD. The age group with the highest prevalence of chlamydia is fifteen- to nineteen-year-olds. One in ten adolescents and one in five sexually active adults are currently infected. Chlamydia usually begins with no symptoms. Sometimes an infected person may experience pain and discharge. The disease lasts around fifteen months, after which time the body then rids itself of the infection unless the person becomes reinfected. Twenty to forty percent of those with untreated chlamydia will develop pelvic inflammatory disease (PID). PID can lead to infertility problems later on in life. In fact, twenty-five to thirty percent of all infertility is related to

## Things You Should Know

chlamydia. The risk of ectopic (tubal) pregnancy increases with each successive infection. Chlamydia can also cause some infertility complications in men. Chlamydia is a curable bacterial infection that can be diagnosed with a urine test, but because it has so few symptoms, the damage it causes may be complete before it is detected. There is insufficient data to confirm that condoms are effective to prevent chlamydia. The other top bacterial STDs are gonorrhea (650,000 new cases each year), syphilis, trichomoniasis and bacterial vaginitis. Birth control pills do not prevent bacterial infections.[2]

We hear a lot about HIV, the virus that causes AIDS. Deadly and incurable, this disease hogs the headlines. But it is actually far more likely that your sexually active child will encounter two other viral STDs long before exposure to HIV. Human papilloma virus (HPV), also called genital warts, is now the most common *viral* STD (5.5 million new cases in the U.S. each year), and most teens have never even heard of it. In fact, twenty percent of American women have been infected at least once in their lifetime. There are 100 different types of HPV, thirty of which affect the genital area and are considered to be STDs. HPV causes wart-like growths on the infected area. Most cases are asymptomatic and most are benign. So why should we worry about this infection? Because HPV leads to 99.7 percent of all cervical cancer and more women die of cervical cancer than die of AIDS each year. There are 12,800 cases of cervical cancer in the U.S. each year, causing 4,600 deaths. HPV can also cause cancer in the penis and anus in men.[3]

The age of the woman is a significant factor in her susceptibility to HPV. As young teens mature, the cells in the cervix change rapidly. Young women are most vulnerable to disease and cancer because of these changes. Delaying their sexual "debut" would dramatically decrease their chances of getting cervical cancer. HPV can be detected by a pap smear. Treatment is biopsy and cryogenic surgery. Most birth control methods, including condoms, do not reduce the risk of acquiring HPV. Most frightening is that HPV can be transmitted by fingers, sex toys, oral sex and skin-to-skin contact.[4]

Genital herpes (HSV2) is another viral STD. This year, 1 million people will acquire HSV2, the virus that causes genital herpes. It is so prevalent that an estimated one in five people are currently infected.[5] HSV2 causes outbreaks of painful lesions, periodic eruptions, blisters and ulcers in both men and women. It used to be thought that transmission could only occur during these outbreaks, but studies have revealed that infection can occur even when symptoms are not evident. Commercials are now aired on prime-time TV for prescription medications for genital herpes. But, as the ads indicate, these prescription anti-viral products only treat symptoms—there is no cure for genital herpes. Condoms have been shown to reduce risk only to areas covered by the condom.

## Sex Is Sexist

What makes a person more susceptible to STD infection? Some risk factors are apparent: The number of sexual partners over a lifetime, the number of concurrent partners and the risk profile of those sex partners are good indicators of risk. But age and gender are also key factors. Also, and this is an important point to impress upon young women, sex is sexist: The consequences of sexual activity simply have more impact on women than on men. Physically, emotionally and relationally, women are more vulnerable to damage when they engage in sexual activity. Pregnancy and childbirth are obvious examples of the consequences. Because of the receptive nature of the female anatomy and the changes in the female body taking place during adolescence, teenage girls are at higher risk of infection when sexually active.[6]

To arm yourself with further statistics and other information, you can find a resource catalogue at the Medical Institute for Sexual Health, P.O. Box 162306, Austin, TX 78716, MedInstitute.org. For more information about condom failure, look up the National Institutes of Health condom study at www.niaid.nih.gov/dmid/stds/condomreport.pdf.

## Notes:

1. Joe McIlhaney, Jr., M.D., "Fighting an Epidemic with Wishful Thinking," [on-line], n.d., The Medical Institute. May 8, 2003. Available from: <http://www.medinstitute.org/media/index.htm>.
2. Centers for Disease Control and Prevention, "Tracking the Hidden Epidemics," [on-line], July 3, 2001. May 8, 2003. Available from: <http://www.cdc.gov/nchstp/od/news/RevBrochure1pdftoc.htm#TRENDS%20BY%20DISEASE>.
3. The Medical Institute, "HPV Vaccine Press Release: HPV Vaccine Offers Hope, Also Points Out Seriousness of Epidemic, Says The Medical Institute for Sexual Health," [on-line], November 25, 2002. May 8, 2003. Available from: <http://www.medinstitute.org/media/index.htm>.
4. J.R. Mann, C.C. Stine, J. Vessey, "The Role of Disease Specific Infectivity and the Number of Disease Exposures on Long-Term Effectiveness of the Latex Condom," *Sexually Transmitted Disease*, 2002:20, pp. 344-9.
5. G. Armstrong, J. Schillinger, L. Markowitz, et.al., "Incidence of Herpes Simplex Virus Type 2 Infection in the U.S.," *American Journal of Epidemiology*, 2001:153, pp. 912-20.
6. Mann, et al., pp. 344-9.

# appendix b

Arterburn, Stephen, *Every Man's Battle: Winning the War on Sexual Purity One Victory at a Time*. Colorado Springs, CO: Waterbrook Press, 2000.

———. *Every Woman's Desire: An Every Man's Guide to Winning the Heart of a Woman*. Colorado Springs, CO: Waterbrook Press, 2001.

———. *Every Young Man's Battle: Strategies for Victory in the Real World of Sexual Temptation*. Colorado Springs, CO: Waterbrook Press, 2002.

Chapman, Gary. *The Five Love Languages*. Chicago, IL: Moody Press, 1992.

———. *The Five Love Languages of Teenagers*. Chicago, IL: Moody Press, 2000.

Clark, Jeremy. *I Gave Dating a Chance*. Colorado Springs, CO: Waterbrook Press, 2000.

DeMoss, Robert. *21 Days to Better Family Entertainment*. Grand Rapids, MI: Zondervan Publishing, 1998.

———. *Learn to Discern*. Grand Rapids, MI: Zondervan Publishing, 1997.

Dobson, James. *Bringing Up Boys*. Carol Stream, IL: Tyndale House, 2001.

———. *Preparing for Adolescence*. Ventura, CA: Gospel Light, 1999.

# Helpful Resources

Elliot, Elisabeth. *Passion and Purity: Learning to Bring Your Love Life Under Christ's Control*. Grand Rapids, MI: Baker/Revell, 2002.

Gresh, Dannah. *And the Bride Wore White: Seven Secrets to Sexual Purity*. Chicago, IL: Moody Press, 2000.

Harris, Joshua. *I Kissed Dating Goodbye: A New Attitude Toward Relationships and Romance*. Sisters, OR: Multnomah Publishers, Inc., 1997.

Hart, Archibald. *The Sexual Man*. Nashville, TN: Thomas Nelson, 1995.

Jones, Stan and Brenna. *Facing the Facts* (Ages 11-14). Colorado Springs, CO: NavPress, 1994.

———. *What's the Big Deal? Why God Cares About Sex* (Ages 8-11). Colorado Springs, CO: NavPress, 1994.

Lewis, Robert. *Raising a Modern-Day Knight*. Colorado Springs, CO: Focus on the Family, 1999.

Nystrom, Carolyn. *Before I Was Born*. Colorado Springs, CO: NavPress, 1994.

Speck, Greg. *Sex: It's Worth Waiting For*. Chicago, IL: Moody Press, 1989.

White, Joe. *Faith Training: Raising Kids Who Love the Lord*. Colorado Springs, CO: Focus on the Family, 1996.

———. *Pure Excitement: A Radical, Righteous Approach to Sex, Love and Dating*. Colorado Springs, CO: Focus on the Family, 1996.

## Web Sites:

www.medinstitute.org—*up-to-date information on STDs.*

www.truelovewaits.com—*purity pledge committment information.*

www.getthetruth.net—*medically accurate and timely news and support for people who are concerned about the sexual health of young people.*

www.silverringthing.com—*purity pledge programs.*